The
Thorn
of
Sexual
Abuse

THE
THORN
OF
SEXUAL
ABUSE

The Gripping Story
of a Family's Courage
and One Man's Struggle

BETH STERLING

Fleming H. Revell
A Division of Baker Book House Co
Grand Rapids, Michigan 49516

© 1994 by Beth Sterling

BV4460.8
.S74
1994

Published by Fleming H. Revell
a division of Baker Book House Company
P.O. Box 6287, Grand Rapids, MI 49516-6287

Printed in the United States of America

Library of Congress Cataloging-in-Publication Data

Sterling, Beth.
The thorn of sexual abuse: the gripping story of a family's courage and one man's struggle / Beth Sterling.
p. cm.
ISBN 0-8007-5500-6
1. Sex addicts—Pastoral counseling of—Case studies. 2. Sex addicts—Religious life. 3. Sex addiction—Religious aspects—Christianity. 4. Child molesters—Pastoral counseling of—Case studies. 5. Child molesters—Religious life. 6. Child sexual abuse—Religious aspects—Christianity. 7. Sex addicts—Family relationships—Case studies. 8. Child molesters—Family relationships—Case studies. 9. Family—Religious life. 10. Sterling, Beth. I. Title.
BV4460.8.S74 1994
261.8'32—dc20   93-33320

Unless otherwise noted, Scripture quotations are taken from *The Living Bible*, copyright © 1971 by Tyndale House Publishers, Wheaton, Illinois. Used by permission.

Gratitude is expressed for permission to use material from the following:

Out of the Shadows, Copyright © 1983 Patrick J. Carnes. Published by CompCare Publishers, Minneapolis, MN.

Retraining Adult Sex Offenders: Methods and Models, Copyright © 1984 by Fay Honey Knopp. Published by Safer Society Press. (Permission granted by individual writers.)

Treating Child Sex Offenders and Victims, by Anna C. Salter, Copyright © 1988 by Sage Publications, Inc.

You Don't Have to Molest That Child, by Timothy A. Smith, Copyright © 1987 by the National Committee for the Prevention of Child Abuse.

To all those who suffer silently behind closed doors.

There is a way out!

Contents

Preface   9
Introduction   13

1   How Can We Help?   15
2   He Hugs Me "Funny"   21
3   Stranger in Our Midst   30
4   A Matter of Trust   38
5   Cheese and Nonsense   44
6   The Friend with Many Faces   50
7   Filthy Rags   57
8   Tears and Forgiveness   63
9   Sexual Addiction—What Is It?   78
10   Child Molestation   87
11   The Arraignment   92
12   Excuses and Symptoms   107
13   Diagnosis   113
14   Marie's Search for Herself   126
15   The Sentencing   131
16   Rebuilding a Marriage   137
17   The Treatment   148
18   In Recovery   161

Epilogue   167
A Professional Perspective   169
Sources of Help   175
Notes   177

Preface

This is the true story of one man's struggle to overcome his sexual addiction. He is a convicted child molester who is now in recovery. It is also the story of a woman who, as a child, was sexually abused. This narrative describes the interaction between these two people and their families.

Many people believe that sexual behavior is simply a matter of willpower or choice. The idea that a person can be addicted to sex—that it is an illness—is new to them. It is not new, however, to the professionals who treat it. They know it is only another of the many addictive ways that people use to escape their internal pain, isolation, lack of trust, secretiveness, loneliness, tension, insecurity, and emotional problems. It also provides them with a false sense of power. Sex addicts are searching for something that cannot be found in their addiction—emotional and spiritual security.

Sexual addiction does not respect any particular race, age, sex, ethnic group, nationality, or social status. It can be found in people from all walks of life. In all probability you have at least one friend who suffers from this illness. If you have tried to stop lustful, sexual behavior or to end a sexual relationship and found you couldn't, you may be a sex addict. A sex addict is a person who knows he or she should stop—but can't.

Nationwide scientific studies indicate that a significant portion of the population have experienced at least one incidence of childhood sexual abuse. Just as many people feel that sexual behavior is simply a matter of willpower or choice, many also believe that the nonviolent sexual abuse of a child, while wrong, leaves no permanent scars. This is not true! All abuse, whether sexual, physical, or emotional always causes damage. Ironically, the child carries into adulthood the same things that the sex addict does: internal pain, isolation, loneliness, tension, lack of trust, secretiveness, insecurity, and emotional problems. Sexually abused children and sex addicts both grow up searching for emotional and spiritual security in inappropriate and destructive ways.

Denying the existence of sexual addiction and the prevalence of childhood sexual abuse will not make these problems go away. Being properly informed, and then using such information in a positive and constructive way can make a difference.

It is the fervent prayer of all who have been involved in the writing and publication of this book that the contents will provide help, hope, and inspiration to the millions of persons who quietly struggle every day of their lives with sexual addiction and/or the consequences of sexual abuse.

Existing studies indicate that, statistically, more female children are abused than male children and that more males are sexual offenders/sexual addicts than females. This is not to imply that only female children are abused, since surely they are not, nor that only males are sex offenders/sex addicts, since surely they are not. For simplification, however, female pronouns will be used primarily in this book to describe adult females and sexually abused children, while male pronouns will be used to describe sexual offenders and sexual addicts.

While "Paul," on the recommendation of his counselor, chose a specific twelve-step group, he did so because it suited his needs. It is not the intent of this book, its authors, or publishers to either endorse or oppose any specific twelve-step group for sexual addiction.

This is a true story and all persons mentioned are real; their names have been changed to protect their anonymity.

I want to thank the following individuals for their prayers, editing skills, encouragement, and professional contributions: Dick, Herb, Pastor John, Glenda, Jane, Wayne, Judy, Mary, Janine, Norman, Lily, and Jack.

Introduction

As you read *The Thorn of Sexual Abuse*, I hope that you will see not only the words but also the very real and honest people who are sharing their intimate thoughts and feelings with you.

This book is about sexual addiction and a convicted child molester who, after being sexually abused as a child, became the abuser.

Some may feel that portions of this book are too graphic. The intent is not to titillate or amuse but, rather, to describe the child molester, or potential molester, so he or she may recognize himself or herself and seek help. It is also my prayer that victims of childhood sexual abuse can identify with Paul's victims or with this author and realize that the abuse they endured was not their fault and that they also should seek help. Try to read the book through the eyes of those involved and experience it with your emotions.

This is a powerful book, written by a victim of childhood sexual abuse, in collaboration with a sex offender. The pain Paul and I experienced as we talked and confronted one another is evident and, at times, heartbreaking. But, by being willing to openly and honestly share, we both found God's healing, forgiveness, and a new friend.

The incidence of all sex crimes is steadily increasing—not only against children of both sexes but also against adults. More has to be done to address this major problem. People are justifiably angry, but such anger is wasted unless it is properly channeled so that it brings about positive change. We need to pray for increased awareness, education, and understanding; improved legislation; and better treatment programs for sexual offenders, sex addicts, and victims of childhood abuse.

· 1 ·

How Can We Help?

*If they fall it isn't fatal, for the Lord holds them
with his hand.*

Psalm 37:24

It was early on a Sunday morning in July when we received the call. Doug, my husband, reached automatically for the telephone beside our bed. *Well*, I thought, *it's almost time to get up anyway if we're going to make it to the early church service.*

Doug, who had mumbled a sleepy "hello" to the caller, suddenly seemed to be wide awake. He was listening intently with a worried look on his face. This look quickly changed to disbelief. When he finally spoke, his voice was gentle. "Marie," he asked, "do you have an attorney?"

When I heard the word *attorney*, I became concerned. *What was going on?* The only Marie I knew was from a small church we had previously attended. Although Marie's husband, Paul, and Doug both served as church deacons, we hadn't socialized with them except at church-related activities.

Doug was being cautious with his words. "Marie, is there a possibility—even a remote one—that Paul could be guilty?"

Guilty of what? I wondered. *Had there been a car accident? Had he been speeding?* Whatever the problem, I was sure that it couldn't be really serious.

Finally, Doug asked, "How can we help?"

There was a brief pause, and then my husband spoke again. "Of course she can stay here. I'll talk to Beth, but I'm sure we can work it out."

"What will we work out?" I asked, as he placed the receiver on the hook. "What's going on?"

"Paul's in jail. His bail has been set at fifty thousand dollars."

I gasped, "Fifty thousand! What did he do?"

"It was hard to understand what Marie was trying to tell me, but apparently he's been charged with sexually molesting two young girls. She also said something about him using the telephone to conduct a sex survey. The police informed her that they had traced the calls back to their home phone number."

"No," I said. "It's impossible! There's no way he'd do anything like that!"

"Honey, it sounds as if the police have hard evidence."

"But we know him—he's a Christian."

"Beth, does anyone ever really know what's going on inside another person's mind? We only see what they allow us to see—nothing more. Even Christians have problems."

Tina, our twenty-year-old daughter, came bursting into our room. "Why are you guys up so early?" Pushing her long, blond hair away from her eyes she complained, "I wanted to sleep in this morning!"

Her dad told her about the phone call and what little we knew about the situation. "No way," she said. "I don't believe it! He's super with the kids at church. . . . And besides, he has a young daughter."

Her words set off an inner alarm! "You don't suppose he's abused Ann?" I gasped.

"I pray not," Doug said, "but Marie did ask me if Ann could come to live with us for a while. She's afraid that the Child Welfare Agency might intervene and place her in a foster home. For now, she's taken Ann to live with her cousin who lives a couple of hours away."

Marie must be devastated, I thought. *She needs her daughter close to her.* Aloud I said, "I think we can manage that. Thank God, my business office is in our home."

"I doubt if she even remembers that you have a business," Doug said. "She's only worried about losing her daughter— even temporarily."

There was no way I could visualize that happening. I wasn't a social worker, but Ann, with her impish smile, sparkling brown eyes, and outgoing personality didn't appear to be abused in any way. She was, perhaps, a bit spoiled, but I understood how that could easily happen with a late-in-life baby. Her brother and sister were both grown and on their own.

"I think we should get dressed for church," Doug said. "We need to pray for their family. I can't forget the way Marie sounded on the phone. If this nightmare is true, I'm convinced she didn't know that Paul was doing these things. She sounded totally devastated."

While kneeling at the altar in church, I prayed intensely for Marie, Ann, and the children who were involved. But when I tried to pray for Paul, my heart wouldn't cooperate. I felt a coldness inside that frightened me.

For the next few days, I busily prepared our house for Ann's visit. Our son, Eric, was away at college, so I cleaned his vacant room for her use. Thank God, it was summer and Ann wouldn't have the added worry of school. Still, I knew it wasn't going to be easy—watching a six-year-old, running a publishing company, and studying for my degree in pastoral ministries all at the same time. *Poor Ann*, I thought. *She'll be confused and frightened.* I wondered if she understood what was happening.

Our home is in a small town where Doug works as an engineer for a large company. Ann and her family live approximately thirty miles from us.

As I dusted furniture, cleaned out drawers, and put away the trophies Eric had won for running, I stopped to look at a family picture, which sat on his dresser. It had begun to fade from the passage of time. *Where have the years gone?* I asked myself. Even at thirteen, Eric had such a serious look on his face. The picture reflected his deep blue, inquisitive eyes, perfectly combed brown hair, and a forced smile that was almost imperceptible. Tina, who was two years younger than her brother, looked innocent and vulnerable. Her blond boyish haircut and sparkling eyes—also blue—were a reflection of her father. I shuddered, realizing that at the time of the photo she was approximately the same age as the girls Paul had allegedly touched.

When Doug and I read the newspaper account of Paul's arrest, it was unnerving. The printed words made it all too real:

> A 49-year-old man has been charged with multiple counts of sexual misconduct involving juvenile girls and with conducting a bogus telephone sex survey also aimed at young girls. He waived his right to a preliminary hearing yesterday before District Justice Andrew Bixler.
>
> The accused is charged with 6 counts of indecent assault . . . and disorderly conduct in connection with incidents July 8 and 15 involving girls at an area swimming pool. He is also charged with three counts of harassment by communication for allegedly calling young girls . . . identifying himself as a

representative of The American Education Institute, questioning them about their knowledge of sexual practices.

Again I thought about Ann, praying that she hadn't been abused by her father. If so, she would need professional help!

"Oh, God," I said aloud, "I don't need this. It brings back too many memories—feelings I don't want to remember and don't know how to deal with. Forgive me for not really wanting Ann to come here. None of this is her fault!"

As it turned out, she didn't come to stay with us. Paul, who had been released on bail, called to inform us that there had been a change in plans.

His monotone voice sounded like a programmed recording of information. "Ann's coming home," he said, "and, as long as I'm not living in the house, she can stay with her mom."

His words, "as long as I'm not living in the house," gave me an uneasy feeling, but I tried to hide this and sound enthusiastic. "That's great," I said. "They need to be together."

"It's working out well—we've even found a baby-sitter to watch Ann while Marie is at work."

I'd forgotten that Marie worked full-time as a practical nurse. *Staying busy will probably be good for her,* I thought.

"We do have one problem, though," Paul continued. "I need a place to stay where there aren't any children under eighteen years of age. And since you and Doug have offered to help, I thought maybe you might allow me to stay with you until my case is heard by the court."

"Stay with us?" My voice was guarded. "But you'll be more than thirty miles from your family! Shouldn't you try to find a place nearer home?"

"No, just the opposite!" he said. "As far as the courts are concerned, the farther I am from Ann the better. I've already caused enough grief for my wife; she couldn't handle losing Ann. But, Beth, I'll understand if it isn't convenient for you and Doug. I can always make other arrangements."

"Paul, I . . ."

"If you'll let me stay with you, I'll work. I'm a good painter—and can paint your house for you. Doug used to tell me at church how the workload at his office kept him from doing all the things he needed to do around the house."

What Paul was saying was definitely true. After working at his engineering job all day, Doug came home and worked for our publishing business. The two jobs didn't leave time for him to do anything else.

"I don't think we'll have a problem," I said, "but I have to talk it over with Doug. I'll ask him to call you tonight."

"Thanks, Beth. And if he agrees, I'll move in tomorrow."

"That . . . that'll be fine, Paul." Inwardly, I felt like a hypocrite, realizing that all I wanted to do was to end our conversation. Doug could deal with Paul—maybe even find a tactful way to get us out of this.

As I hung up the phone, I sensed that Paul had also felt relieved when our conversation ended.

If we're this uncomfortable talking on the phone, I thought, *how could we possibly live together in the same house?*

✦ 2 ✦

He Hugs Me "Funny"

Reach down from heaven and rescue me; deliver me from
deep waters, from the power of my enemies.
Psalm 144:7

Feeling sick to my stomach, I went into the living room and collapsed on the couch. As I lay there watching the blades of the ceiling fan going around and around, thinking about what Paul had been accused of, I felt myself being pulled back to the past—back to a day at the lake when I was eleven years old . . .

I had gone there with Janice, my best friend, who lived across the street from me. We had been invited by Tom and Ethel Stephens, neighbors and good friends of my parents. Their son Gary, who was a couple of years younger than I, had missed many classes at school because of his heart condition. My parents asked me to take his homework to him every day, and to stay and visit for awhile in an effort to cheer him up. At first I didn't mind, believing it a great opportunity to trade comic books and enjoy Mrs. Stephens's freshly baked pies. Gary's mom was always very nice to me. I considered the invitation for us to join them in a picnic at the lake to be their way of saying thanks for helping their son.

I hesitated before telling my parents about the invitation, because I wasn't sure if I really wanted to go. Near the end of the school year, Gary's dad had started to treat me differently; he always seemed to be hugging me in a funny way that made me feel uncomfortable. For example, when Gary left the room and his mother was in the kitchen, Mr. Stephens would come into the dining room and hug me.

Mr. Stephens's actions became predictable. "Hi, Sweetie," he'd say, coming up behind my chair and throwing his arms around me. When he did this, his hands would, as if by accident, brush against my breasts, which had just begun to develop. I recall him laughing as I tried to squirm away from his touch. If I happened to be standing when he came into the room, he would "accidentally" fondle my backside until I managed to wiggle away from him.

Being extremely shy, I pulled away, but I never dared say anything to him. Something inside told me that what he was doing was wrong, but I had been taught by my parents to "respect an adult at any cost." I didn't know what to do about his touches, especially since my parents were so proud of me for helping Gary. Unlike my sister Barbara, who excelled in school, sports, and music, I was an average student and felt that I had no special talents or abilities. She always received praise and compliments, while I rarely did. As a result, I was obsessed with trying to please my parents and anxious to receive their approval.

Secretly, I wanted Mr. Stephens's wife to catch him teasing me—at least, that's what he called it. But he was clever! Whenever he heard someone coming, he would take a book from the bookcase or open a desk drawer as if searching for something. Then, when it became time for me to leave for home, he would give me a big good-bye hug in front of his wife and son, as if to assure me that everything he had done was okay. Inwardly, I didn't buy his assurances but convinced myself that I could dodge his unwanted touches until the end of the school year. After that, I promised myself that I wouldn't go near their house ever again.

Although I found it terribly embarrassing to talk about, once I shyly tried, in an awkward way, to tell my mom and dad about Mr. Stephens's hugging me too closely; but they didn't take me seriously. Maybe I wasn't specific enough. Anyway, Dad looked at Mom and said, "Tom is just a friendly person; he loves children." My mom nodded her head in agreement. And so the matter was put to rest as far as my parents were concerned. After all, this man was the nice guy of the neighborhood—an outstanding civic leader—he couldn't possibly have done anything wrong!

When the picnic invitation came, I convinced myself that it would be okay to go. After all, Mrs. Stephens and Gary would be there. And Janice and I would be together. Surely nothing could happen!

Mom was concerned because I didn't know how to swim, but Mrs. Stephens assured her I would be safe. "Tom's an excellent swimmer; the kids will be in good hands," she said.

I knew why Mom was worried; the previous summer I had almost drowned in a pond near my grandmother's house. Although falling off the large, slippery rock into the pond had been bad enough, the most terrifying memory was when I hit the water and thrashed around, totally out of control. I tried to hold my breath, only to take in mouthfuls of dirty water. It felt as though my lungs would burst. Every time I rose to the surface, I could hear the screams of the other kids, including my sister, who were looking down at me from the rock. I was sure I was about to die, and would have if my cousin Bill hadn't come to my rescue. Thank God he was there!

The near-drowning incident was still fresh in my mind. *Don't worry, Mom*, I thought. *I won't go near the water.*

It turned out to be a beautiful day for a picnic; we were at a secluded and private area of the lake. After filling up on hot dogs, potato salad, and chocolate cake, Janice and I sat on the beach, chatting and giggling about anything and everything. The two of us were a lot alike, except in looks. Janice, mature for her age, was slightly chubby with thick dark hair, while I was a fair-skinned blond with a toothpick shape.

Janice suddenly stood up. "Come on," she said, "let's go swimming!"

"You go ahead," I replied. "I'll go over and keep Gary company. You know he isn't allowed to swim because of his heart condition."

"C'mon, you can keep him company later; let's swim now while we have the chance. Besides, he's busy building a sand castle."

I didn't want to admit to her that I was afraid of the water. One thing that never changes from generation to generation is the desire to fit in, to have the respect of friends, to belong. "Go ahead," I repeated. "I'm just not in the mood for swimming."

She became annoyed. "You didn't go in the pool when we went with the church group either. What's wrong? Are you chicken?"

"No, I'm not chicken. But . . . well, I don't know how to swim." I started to tell her about the near-drowning incident, but she interrupted.

"So what! I can't swim very well either, but we can toss the ball around in the shallow water. It'll cool us off."

As Mr. and Mrs. Stephens walked toward us, they apparently overheard part of our conversation, because Mr. Stephens made us an offer. "You young ladies should learn how to swim. How about me teaching you?"

"Great!" shouted Janice. "I'll be first!"

"Okay," I reluctantly found myself saying. I was afraid of him and terrified of the water, but didn't want to admit it.

Over and over, I've tried to understand what that eleven-year-old girl was thinking and feeling. Why was she so trusting—so quick to forget how this man had repeatedly touched her?

As he led Janice into the deep water, I began to take off the outer clothing that I had worn over my swimsuit. Then, with my heart pounding, I approached the water's edge and walked into the lake. *This isn't so bad,* I thought. *Maybe after today, I won't fear the water anymore.* After a few minutes I sat down and began scooping up water in my hands, splashing it around until my entire swimsuit was wet—getting used to the water gradually.

When Janice's lesson was over, Mr. Stephens brought her to where I was and cautioned her, "You've only had one lesson, so don't try and swim in the deep water without me." Then he added in a stern voice, "Remember the other things I warned you about!"

Without saying a word, she ran to where Gary was playing on the beach. I fearfully clutched Mr. Stephens's hand as he took me into the deep water. Then, supporting me in his arms, he taught me how to kick and move my arms. I was trying to do what he wanted when, suddenly, I panicked and began to flounder. "I'm scared," I said. "I want to go back!"

"Honey, relax. I won't let anything happen to you."

"I mean it," I said loudly. "I want to go back! Right now!"

"Okay, okay, Beth, calm down; I'll take you back," he said, helping me to stand. "Look, the water is barely touching your shoulders. You're safe here."

223883

His words and the sand under my feet made me feel better—but only a little. "I . . . I still want to go back."

And so we slowly began walking back toward the shore. Again, I tightly gripped his hand while concentrating on how much farther we had to go. Suddenly, I felt his free hand pressing against my stomach, moving downward in a circular motion, and then fondling me in an intimate place. *This man is definitely not my friend*, I thought.

"Stop doing that," I said, turning to face him. "I don't like it." He looked at me with a strange expression on his face. "Please," I said, "stop touching me there. It feels funny, and I don't like it!"

He stopped and slowly removed his hand, then spoke with agitation. "If you don't like my touching you, then why did you come here today?"

"Because—because, I like picnics," I said, near tears. "And my parents told me that you're a 'nice' person." What I said sounded crazy, even to me!

"Beth, I am a nice person, and so are you. Don't you know that I like you? You shouldn't be ashamed of your body, in fact, you should enjoy being touched. There's so much—so much—that I can teach you. When people like each other, they touch each other in special places. It feels good—real good. Once you've tried it, you'll really like it!"

Oh, no! I thought. *Why did I come here today? What else is he going to do to me? If I yell for help, everyone will be mad at me. Mrs. Stephens will hate me, and Gary will say I'm lying. And my parents—I don't want them to be ashamed of me. Somehow, this must be my fault! I'll be blamed!*

Mr. Stephens, sensing my confusion and turmoil, took advantage of the moment. Placing one arm around my waist, he slid his other hand underneath the edge of the bottom of my bathing suit. As he began touching my private area, I stood there terrified, trying to pretend this wasn't happening. It seemed as if the touching went on forever but, in reality, it probably wasn't more than a minute or two. I felt ugly, dirty, and ashamed—unable to understand why he was doing this to me. *Did he sense something bad about me?* Also, his touches, although unwanted, awakened in me a strange new sensitivity about my body, which caused me even more confusion and guilt.

Finally he stopped! It was over! Mr. Stephens was breathing heavily when he said, "Now, Beth, that wasn't so bad, was it?"

Afraid of angering him, I didn't say anything until we were closer to the beach. Then I expressed my rage. "I hate you— I really hate you! I'm never coming near you again!"

"You don't mean that."

"Yes, I do . . . and . . . I'm going to tell my parents . . . your wife . . . everyone!"

"Who will believe you?" Without giving me a chance to reply, he continued. "Absolutely no one—you're just a kid." His voice became threatening. "If you do tell, you'll be the one who gets in trouble. Kids who tell lies about other people get punished."

He let me go and, as soon as my feet touched the sandy beach, I ran up to his wife. "Mrs. Stephens," I said, "I want to go home, I'm sick to my stomach."

"I want to go, too," Janice said. "My grandparents are coming to visit this evening."

They didn't try to change our minds. I think Mrs. Stephens was concerned about Gary's health, that he might have overdone it by playing for so long in the hot sun.

As we drove to town, we barely spoke. The return ride was certainly different than the drive to the lake had been; we had all laughed, joked, and sung as we looked forward to the joyful day ahead.

The next day, when Janice and I were talking, we found out that Mr. Stephens had touched both of us in the same intimate way.

"Are you going to tell your mom and dad?" I asked.

"No," she said. "I would *never* tell them! I don't want them to know."

I felt the same way—yet, a part of me wanted to confess to my mom and dad what had happened. *Maybe, if I told them about it, I wouldn't feel so bad inside.*

About three weeks later, Mom asked me to take a package to Mrs. Stephens. It was evening, so I was sure that Mr. Stephens would be home.

"Mom, I'm too busy to go over there."

"Well, Miss high and mighty, that's just too bad! You're not the only one who's busy. You're going!"

"Please, Mom," I begged, "don't make me go! When we were at the lake Mr. Stephens did creepy and bad things to me. I hate him!"

Her voice softened. "Did he give you another of those funny hugs?"

"No—it was worse. He put his hand inside my bathing suit and touched me." I began to cry.

Mom took me in her arms. "It's okay," she said, sympathetically. "You don't have to go. I want you to stay away from him. Did he do anything else to you?"

"No, he just touched me. I'm sorry, Mama . . . so sorry! Am I bad?"

I could tell she was uncomfortable but, in her own way, she was being there for me. "Honey, don't talk about it anymore—just put it out of your mind. You're a good girl."

Still crying, I said, "I just don't understand why he touched me there—why he did it."

"When you're a little older, you'll understand." She hesitated before continuing. "I was about your age when a minister touched me the same way. My mom and dad, your grandparents, left me alone in the living room with him. He told me he had brought me some candy, but I would have to climb on his lap and reach into his pants pocket to get it. So I did what he asked—that's when it happened."

"What did he do?"

Her face flushed. "He started feeling me."

"But it wasn't your fault!"

"I know, but I willingly sat on his lap," she said soberly. "Afterwards, I threw the candy away. I never told anyone."

Mom and I never talked about either experience again, and I had no further contact with the Stephens.

Why, oh why, I thought, *did Paul have to call and trigger these memories, which I had tried to bury in my mind for so long?*

✦ 3 ✦

Stranger in Our Midst

*For I was hungry and you fed me; I was thirsty
and you gave me water; I was a stranger
and you invited me into your homes.*
Matthew 25:35

When Doug arrived home from work, I anxiously met him at the door. Startling words, not my customary kiss, greeted him. "It's . . . it's Paul," I stammered. "*He* called and asked if he could come and live with us until he's sentenced."

"*He*," Doug echoed. "What about Ann?"

"She'll be staying with her mother," I said.

Doug fixed tea, and as we sat at the kitchen table drinking it, I shared the details of Paul's call. Through our many years of marriage, it had become a tradition for us to have tea at our kitchen table whenever we discussed important matters.

"What are we going to do?" I asked. "What will we tell him?"

He sighed, "I don't know. This changes everything. I'm concerned for Tina—even if his problem does seem to involve only young girls."

My body tensed, responding to inner anger. "You needn't worry," I said. "If we do decide to let Paul stay here, I won't give him any opportunities to try anything with her. I'm not the same trusting, eleven-year-old girl who went to the lake."

"Hey Beth," Doug said, reaching across the table to take my hand. "Calm down, we're talking about Paul and our daughter, not you and Tom Stephens."

His words made me uncomfortable. "I know who we're talking about," I replied defensively. "It's just that . . . well, why didn't he just rob a bank?"

"That would be funny," Doug said, "if what we're talking about wasn't so darn serious. But the truth is, if he comes to stay with us, we'll be sharing our home with an accused child molester."

"Do you think he'll go to jail?"

"Who knows? Your guess is as good as mine! But, with all the sexual abuse cases on TV and in the newspapers, it seems the courts have really begun to crack down on sex offenders."

"It's about time they started to crack down on them! It scares me to think about what's going on in the world."

"At least Paul has been stopped. If he's sick—and I'm sure he is—I hope they don't just throw him in jail. He needs treatment."

"First things first! He could be with us for several months before he's sentenced. Remember, I once worked as a legal secretary; I know about court calendars and delays."

"So, Beth, what do you think? Can *you* handle it? Can *we* handle it? Remember, Paul took an early retirement from his government job; he'll be with us twenty-four hours a day."

"He'll be outside most of the time."

"What about when it rains?"

"Oh, I don't know. I guess he could read . . . or maybe watch TV. I'll be busy working in my office downstairs. And besides, it doesn't really matter because there'll usually be other people around. You know—my office help, clients . . ."

"Don't forget about our daughter," he interjected. "With her irregular work schedule at the beauty shop, she'll be coming and going at all hours. What will you do—run upstairs to protect her every time she comes home?"

"No, but I'll tell her she's never to be alone with him. And, I'll make sure I know where they are whenever they're in the house together."

"Sounds as though you've already given some thought to this and got all the bases covered! That's good; we need to know exactly what we're getting into!"

"What we're getting into!" I repeated. "Are you saying that he can stay with us?"

"Yes, but only if it's alright with you, Beth. What do you think?"

"I'm uneasy—very uneasy—but I'm willing to give it a try." I paused. "But, if there's any trouble, out he goes!"

When the doorbell rang the next afternoon, I steeled myself. *Help me, God—Help us*, I murmured as I invited Paul into our living room.

We stood there awkwardly facing one another, trying to think of something appropriate to say. Because Paul always appeared to be outgoing and self-assured, I assumed he was a person very much in control of his life. The confidence with which he carried his five-foot-ten-inch stockily built frame further enhanced the positive image I had of him.

Paul's fingers tightly gripped the handle of his suitcase.

"You can take your suitcase to your room," I said, pointing to the door that led to the hallway. "Turn right and then it's the first room on your left."

"Thanks, Beth." Then, in an apologetic voice, he added, "I have another suitcase in the car. But that's it—I only brought the essentials."

As he carried in his second suitcase, I said, "I'm afraid your room is small and doesn't have much storage space."

"Beth," he said reassuringly, "the room is fine. After four nights in jail, it looks like the presidential suite."

"Can I fix you some lunch before I go down to my office?"

"No thanks. I've already eaten—I'm just anxious to start working. Do you know where Doug keeps his pruning shears and hedge clippers?"

"They should be in the garage," I said. "Go out through the kitchen door."

He started to walk toward the door, then stopped and turned to face me. For the first time since his arrival, we made eye contact.

"Beth," he said. "I don't want you to worry; I . . . I swear, I'll never hurt you—not in any way."

My response was immediate. "Paul, I'm not concerned about *me*; my concern is for Tina. I . . . I don't want you alone with her—ever! It doesn't matter what you have or haven't done—it's the way it has to be!"

"I understand," he said as he went out into the garage.

Paul did everything possible to avoid getting in our way. Every day, from morning till night, he did yard work, pruned trees, cut firewood, and scraped our house in preparation for painting. It was work, work, work! The only time he stopped was to eat a quick lunch, get a drink of water, and use the bathroom. He was like a mechanical superman who was wound so tightly that one additional twist would break the spring. And yet, I sensed that this frenzied schedule of activity was his lifeline—a way for him to maintain sanity. "He acts like he's trying to self-destruct," Tina commented.

"Or maybe just running from himself," I replied.

Paul's hazel eyes reflected the turmoil in his life. They would dart back and forth, side to side, scanning things, but never lingering in one place long enough to really see what was there. Most of the time he was quiet and appeared depressed, but then, every so often, he would behave as if he were high on a drug, talking nonstop about every subject imaginable. During these high times he would assume a superior attitude, dominate the conversation, and try to control the person or situation. Often he would abruptly and inappropriately lose his temper. Eventually I came to recognize a definite pattern or cycle in these changes of personality.

Any person seeing the four of us eating our evening meal would have observed what outwardly appeared to be a typical family. We took turns saying the blessing and, when it was Paul's turn, he sounded humble and sincere. *Is he conning us?* I wondered. *If he's a Christian, how could he have done the things he's been accused of?*

Between "pass the potatoes," and "have some more coffee," we made polite conversation, which became a little easier each day. Occasionally, Paul would relax enough to laugh or joke about something. For some reason this infuriated me. *How dare you act happy!* I'd say to myself. *You should be worrying about going to jail!* Sometimes, when I'd look across the table, I'd momentarily see Tom Stephens sitting there instead of Paul.

Forgive me, Lord, I'd pray. *Doug and I have opened our home in Christian love, but my heart isn't responding. Oh, I speak to him, cook for him, and do his laundry; but emotionally I continue to judge and reject him.*

Paul's rigorous nonstop workday was, by necessity, changed as he made frequent trips back to his hometown and the surrounding area. He had to see his physicians, consult with his attorney, visit his Christian therapist, and attend group support meetings for people with sexual problems. He had been diagnosed as having a sexual addiction—something I'd never heard of.

On the advice of his counselor, he began to keep a daily log of his activities in order to account for every minute of his time. He would write down the names of people he saw wherever he went so that, if necessary, they could be his witnesses. The possibility always existed that someone might bring additional charges, legitimate or otherwise, against him. When he was with us, we were his alibi, but whenever he left, he had to be extra cautious. If a meeting lasted longer than planned, he called to let us know what time to expect him.

During the trips to his hometown, Paul learned what it was like to be hated. Former friends crossed the street to avoid speaking to him. Others called him names or made threats about what they would like to do to him and his family. Many believed he should be in jail or—better yet—castrated! After all, he stood accused of committing one of the most horrible crimes known to society. As a defense, he would put on his "I don't care what you say; you can't bother me" attitude, which upset the people even more. Just like me, they expected him to act ashamed and guilty. Perhaps if they had followed him back to our house, they would have seen what they were looking for. Sometimes he would be quiet and despondent for days. Work became his outlet for pain, frustration, and depression. Yes, as I came to know him better, I began to recognize that he was in pain.

The pain that I recognized in Paul was also reflected in Marie's face. I considered her to be an attractive woman—a modern-day Mona Lisa. Although she was continually trying to lose twenty pounds, her light brown hair and wide-set, expressive, deep brown eyes drew looks of approval from both sexes. She had always projected an aura of innocence and vulnerability, but now she was facing a devastating reality. Her innocence was shattered, her vulnerability exposed. She was in pain—terrible pain! *Could she ever forgive Paul? I wondered. Would she want to continue in a sexual relationship with him?*

Marie started seeing a Christian counselor and attending a small church near their home. In it, she found support and love. She also found a caring Christian family who agreed to baby-sit Ann for her whenever she had to work. Outside of the church, she was often assailed by people's accusations and attacks, but her initial numbness had become a protective wall to hide behind. Every day she would wake, dress, fix breakfast for Ann, take her to the baby-sitter's, and go to work. She lived each day with a robot-like response to people and situations.

On Sunday Paul would go with us to a church we had recently joined. We didn't know any of the people at this church, and quite frankly, this pleased us because we didn't have to explain his presence.

Even though this hurting family couldn't go to church together, I'm sure that the worship and fellowship was extremely important—especially in those crucial early days after Paul's arrest.

I reflected on a similar situation that occurred in a church I attended as a child. A man, faithful to the work of the church, was accused of sexual involvement with a young girl from the Sunday school. It was a horrible scandal! The man, his wife, and son were all tried and convicted, then ignored by God's people. My young mind was confused because I had sat there in my pew, Sunday after Sunday, listening to our minister tell us how God had sent his son, Jesus, to die on a cross for our sins. And yet, for this accused man, all I saw was a finger of condemnation pointed at him and his family by the people of the church. I surmised that there must be some sins that were too bad to be covered by Christ's cross. During that time, God shrank right before my eyes as I watched this desperate, broken family leave town, deserted by church and friends. A few months later, I heard that the man had died, leaving behind his grieving wife and young son.

This incident, so clear in my mind, may have been part of the reason why I wasn't too explicit in telling my parents what had happened when Mr. Stephens sexually abused me several years later. If I had fully exposed him, would he and his family have been destroyed in the same way?

✦ 4 ✦

A Matter of Trust

Trust in the Lord God always, for in the Lord Jehovah is your everlasting strength.

Isaiah 26:4

Marie and Ann visited Paul every weekend in an attempt to maintain a fragment of their family unit. It was obvious that father and daughter loved each other deeply. Although Marie would not allow them to be alone together, they still managed to have a good visit. Ann had been told that her daddy had done some wrong things, but she was too young to fully comprehend what was happening. She had difficulty understanding why Daddy couldn't go home with her when she left.

Marie and Paul spent a few minutes alone during every visit, struggling to find ways to communicate with each other.

Separate counseling sessions were helping them to cope with individual problems, but it was still too soon to tell what effect this would have on their marriage. For now, they had a daughter to protect and help; for her sake, they had to start communicating.

Marie tried to pull herself together, but she had fear in her eyes and anger in her voice. The intensity of her emotional pain and suffering gave her an outward appearance of being physically ill. Oh, how I wanted to convince her that everything would be okay, but, of course, I couldn't—no one could! She was keeping her distance from people, not knowing whom she could trust. *Oh God, help her*, I prayed silently. *Do something.*

Most days were routine. Paul would work outside, Tina would go to the beauty salon, and I, along with my staff, would evaluate and typeset manuscripts. On one particularly busy day, I went upstairs and was surprised to find Tina home from work early. A quick glance at the clock told me that I was wrong—it wasn't early—it was almost time for dinner. And I hadn't even thought about what to fix to eat!

When Paul came in for a drink of water, I brought up the subject of dinner. "I hope you two aren't very hungry," I said.

"I'm starved," Tina replied. "Why?"

"Well, I got so involved in my work that I totally lost track of time." I sighed. "And I still have more work to do."

Paul, who was on one of his infrequent highs, responded with an offer. "Beth, I know that you guys love pizza; how about letting me buy a couple for dinner?"

I had to admit his offer sounded good, but then I remembered that he didn't want to go out into public by himself unless it was absolutely necessary.

He seemed to read my thoughts. "Tina," he said, "why don't you ride with me and show me where the pizza shop is?"

Instantly, I became suspicious. *Why is he asking her to go with him?* I thought. Before she could reply to his question, I answered for her. "She can't go with you. She has a date."

"But, Mom, Dave's not picking me up until 8:30; I have plenty of time."

"Tina, you can't go," I said with authority. "Your room needs to be cleaned, and I suggest you go do it . . . *Now!*"

She didn't say anything, but her departing look was one of protest.

I turned to Paul, trying to appear casual, but my flushed face must have reflected my true feelings. "Thanks for offering, but I'll call Doug and ask him to pick up a pizza on his way home from work."

Paul's look and carefully chosen words told me that he fully understood my concern. "My only intention was to help," he said. "But I don't blame you for wanting to protect your daughter. I really don't! It's okay."

As he went back outside to work, I felt sadness over what had happened, but I also believed that my action was appropriate. I didn't trust him—not with my daughter.

That evening when Doug came home with the pizza, Paul declined to come in and eat with us. "I'm not hungry," he said. "I think I'll skip eating tonight."

I wasn't surprised; my appetite was gone, too!

Marie and Paul continued to live their lives separately, moment by moment, awaiting his arraignment by the court. Their immediate concern was whether or not he would go to jail. His attorney, acting in conjunction with his therapist, was working on a plea bargain with the district attorney. The hope was that in return for a guilty plea, Paul would be placed on probation instead of going to prison. Of course, there was no guarantee that the judge presiding at the arraignment would accept a plea bargain arrangement. Paul told Doug and me that he wasn't guilty of *all* the charges brought against him, but to fight the false charges would result in more adverse publicity and pain for everyone concerned. This was the only reference he made concerning his innocence or guilt. He had to be careful of everything he said to us in case we were called to testify.

Marie and Ann continued to visit with us on weekends, usually accompanied by Shirley, a Christian friend who is best described as a spiritual volcano, ready to erupt and overflow at a moment's notice. She didn't just face reality; she met it frankly and enthusiastically with the full armor of God. After Paul's arrest, her first words to Marie were, "Now, you'll find out who your real friends are."

Before Paul's arrest, Doug and I had never been really close friends with Paul and Marie. We now found ourselves spending a considerable amount of time with this husband and wife who had become virtual strangers to each other. Marie continued to appear wounded. When she did talk, her words were guarded, her voice tense. I kept waiting for her to express her anger toward Paul, but it didn't happen.

As Ann's seventh birthday approached, Marie called and asked if they could have a party for her at our house. She had another special birthday party planned for Ann and her friends, but this would be a family event. Even though Paul had agreed not to be alone with his daughter, he could at least share in the happiness of her birthday.

Realizing that Ann's morale needed a boost, Tina and I decided to try and make her party as festive as possible. We hung streamers and balloons in the dining room, fixed a special meal, and wrapped her presents. Her dad bought her a large stuffed bear—to be named *Cuddles*—and watched us prepare for the party with a puzzled look on his face. He seemed to be asking, *Why are you doing this?*

When the guest of honor arrived with her mother, the mood was lighter than usual. I was pleased to see that Shirley was with them. With more people present it would be less likely for Paul to be left alone with Ann. They were doing everything they could to protect their family unit from court interference. If Paul were never left alone with his daughter, no one could make an accusation against him.

At first the party was great. Ann, caught up in the excitement, enjoyed being the center of attention. Her parents exchanged general conversation, were cordial to each other, and appeared to be more relaxed than on previous visits. Then, late in the afternoon, everything fell apart.

All of us were in the living room drinking birthday punch and watching an old movie on TV. Ann and her dad were sitting on the floor playing tic-tac-toe. Seeing them together in such a typical family scene, I found it difficult to believe the circumstances of their visit.

When they had finished their game, Paul started to stand up. Then Ann, with typical childlike enthusiasm, climbed onto his back saying, "Daddy, give me a piggyback ride!"

Paul started to go along with her request when, suddenly, Marie jumped up, her face ashen. "Ann, no! Stop that! Get off his back! You're getting too big for piggyback rides!"

"No, I'm not, Mom," she replied. "Please, Daddy."

Marie tried another approach. "Ann, how about playing me a game of tic-tac-toe at the dining room table. Bet I can beat you!"

Paul's hands were gently untangling his daughter's arms from around his neck. "Okay, Princess," he said. "Your mom has challenged you. Go beat her!"

Doug, Shirley, and I knew that Paul hadn't done anything wrong—but the festive mood was shattered. Marie had responded with a mother's protective instinct, and we understood that her reaction had been prompted by her inner turmoil. This was a man she had been married to for over a quarter of a century—a man she had loved and believed in. Now, her actions clearly indicated that she felt she couldn't trust him to play with their daughter, even with other people present. My instincts told me that she knew that her husband had never touched their daughter inappropriately, and that she was overreacting because of her fear of what we might think.

Later that evening, Marie told me that Ann had been thoroughly tested and evaluated by psychologists who assured her that their daughter had never been sexually abused. It was the first time she had shared any intimate aspects of the charges with me.

"That's good news," I said, feeling relieved but not surprised. I was cautious with my words. "But, Marie, you still seem very . . . very . . ."

"Watchful," she interjected. "You bet I am. I'm watching every move he makes. I'll never give him an opportunity to touch her!" There was anger in her voice, and her eyes were filled with tears.

Somehow, I knew she had taken a positive step toward her own healing by being able to share information and, even more importantly, her feelings with me.

✦ 5 ✦

Cheese and Nonsense

A cheerful heart does good like medicine,
but a broken spirit makes one sick.
Proverbs 17:22

I t was one of those rare afternoons when I was able to get away from the office—a time spent getting reacquainted with a dust rag, a scrub bucket, and the art of cooking. On this particular day, I had just finished the housework and was busily preparing lasagna—one of our family favorites. The thick tomato sauce was simmering and the noodles were cooked and drained.

I took the container of ricotta cheese out of the refrigerator and removed the lid. My eyes surveyed with disgust the thick layer of grayish green mold on the top. As I spooned into the contents of the container, I found that the mold was not only on the top but all through the cheese. "Darn," I said aloud. "Now, what am I going to do?"

Ricotta cheese wasn't an ingredient I could borrow from a neighbor as easily as I could a cup of flour or sugar. I had to get to a store. But how? If I borrowed Paul's car, he would be alone at the house with no one to verify his whereabouts. Besides, with Tina's irregular work hours, she could come home unexpectedly while I was gone.

If I'm going to get my ricotta, I thought, *Paul will have to drive me to the store.* Looking out the front window, I saw that he was painting our lawn furniture. One thing for sure, Paul's hard work was more than paying for his keep. Remembering Tina and the pizza incident, I felt guilty about asking him to take me. He might refuse, and even if he didn't, I wasn't very thrilled with the idea of being seen in public with him. A few weeks after he'd moved in with us, I went with him to a hardware store to purchase some house paint and a few other things for our home. Having a vivid imagination, I could easily believe that everyone who glanced at us was able to recognize him as a sex offender. These thoughts had continued to run through my mind as we pulled into McDonald's parking lot. When he'd first suggested stopping for coffee, I had hesitated but decided it would be rude to refuse since he had just spent a great deal of money buying house paint. All the time we were in the restaurant, I sat nervously on the edge of my seat, watching the doors, and praying no one who knew me would come in. I felt like a hypocrite—although I'd opened my home to him, I wasn't secure enough to want anyone else to know about it.

The need to have the lasagna ready for dinner overshadowed my misgivings so, taking a glass of water out to Paul, I told him of my dilemma. He didn't hesitate. "Just give me a minute or two to clean up," he said. "Be sure you bring the moldy container of cheese with you. They shouldn't charge you for replacing it."

"I was going to buy a new one. I . . . I really hate to return things. Maybe it's my fault; maybe I kept it too long!"

"Look at the expiration date on the carton."

I checked the date on the bottom of the container, and it verified that the cheese should have still been usable. But I was hesitant because I just didn't like the hassle involved in returning a product. In many ways I was very assertive, but with things like this, I was the original Mrs. Milquetoast—a genuine wimp!

Sensing my feelings, Paul said he would take care of it and exchange it for me. "Why should you pay for something twice? It's not your fault that it's spoiled and can't be used. Besides, stores carry insurance to cover things like breakage and spoilage."

As we drove to the supermarket in silence, every so often I stole a glance at Paul. He appeared so ordinary, so middle class. He just didn't fit my idea of how a sex offender should look. Before his arrest, most people would have described him as being a "good neighbor," a "nice person," an "okay" guy. More than once, when he was unaware of our presence, Doug and I had seen him place bags of groceries into a needy person's car in our church parking lot. Every Sunday morning, he and Marie took turns staying with a sick, elderly man so the man's wife could attend church. They were always reaching out to others. *But*, I thought, *Paul apparently had also been reaching out in inappropriate ways, while professing to be a Christian.* At least the man who molested me hadn't misrepresented himself to others. To my knowledge, my molester seldom, if ever, attended church. *Here I am comparing them again*, I thought. For a fleeting second fear overcame me, and I gripped the door handle tightly, wanting to jump out of the car, wanting to be anywhere except with this man. I closed my eyes and began to pray.

"We're here," he said as he parked his car in the mall parking lot. We entered the store and went straight to the manager's window. Paul authoritatively set the container of cheese on the counter.

A pleasant looking man with premature gray hair came to the window. "May I help you?" he asked.

"We have a problem with your cheese department," Paul said.

"Our cheese department," the man repeated. "That's impossible . . ."

Paul interrupted him by opening the container and saying, "Do you see this mold?"

"I sure do!"

"Would you eat this cheese?"

"No, sir, I wouldn't."

Paul held the container and pointed at the expiration date. "According to this date, it should still be good. Right?"

"It appears so."

"Then you won't mind if we go to your cheese department and exchange this container for a fresh one."

"No, sir, that wouldn't be okay. We don't have a cheese department in our store."

I had stood there quietly listening to their conversation, but now I couldn't remain quiet any longer. "Of course you do; my husband and I buy all our groceries in this store."

He look squarely at Paul. "Your wife is wrong, you couldn't have purchased the cheese here."

Paul looked at me questioningly, but I stood my ground, saying with conviction, "This cheese *did* come from here!"

But the manager was just as insistent. "We carry cheese curls and cheese crackers and cheese snacks, but we don't carry that kind of cheese. I'm afraid we can't help you."

His answer infuriated me. Doug and I had been shopping at this store for years, and now this man was calling me a liar.

As Paul placed the lid on the container, he commented, "This certainly isn't good for your public relations. I thought the customer was always supposed to be right!"

"But you aren't right," the manager said with desperation in his voice. "If we carried cheese, I'd gladly let you exchange it."

He sounded convincing—so much so that Paul questioned me one final time. "Maybe your husband bought the cheese when you weren't with him?"

"There's absolutely no doubt in my mind that I was with him," I said. "I can clearly remember placing the container of cheese in our shopping cart."

The manager had perked up, looking at me with renewed curiosity and interest. He then spoke to Paul, "Oh, so you're not her husband?"

The way he said this—the inflection and tone of voice—caused me to turn in embarrassment and practically run out of the store. As I was leaving I heard the manager loudly say, "Sir, this store doesn't even have a cooler to put cheese in."

A few minutes later, Paul came out of the store and joined me near the car. I was still confused and more than a little embarrassed. "Now what?" he asked.

"I don't know," I said. "I need the cheese, so I guess I'll go back in and buy a new one."

"How can you? The manager said they don't even have a cooler for cheese!"

"That's ridiculous," I said. "Wait here; I'll be right back." As I turned and began to walk toward the entrance, I happened to glance at the name of the store spelled out in big letters above the door. The words didn't register in my mind until I was inside, but once they did, I immediately turned around and went back out the door. Paul, who was still standing by the car, appeared confused, especially when I began to point hysterically at the sign. My words were halted. "Phar-Mor . . . this is Phar-Mor, " I gulped. "Not a supermarket—a large discount pharmacy."

I realized that we must have mistakenly turned off one road ahead of where we should have, putting us in another shopping area, adjacent to, but one street away from the mall where we wanted to be. Phar-Mor was located in this shopping area in the same place as the supermarket was in the main mall. I had been praying with my eyes shut and hadn't been paying attention when we turned into the mall parking lot. And, of course, Paul wasn't familiar with the roads, shopping areas, or store names in our area and assumed he had driven us to the correct place.

He looked at the sign and then at me. Suddenly, he began laughing—none too gently. By this time, the humor in the situation was overpowering me, and I, too, began to laugh. The more we laughed, the funnier it seemed. Paul's voice mimicked mine. "But, sir, my husband and I buy all our groceries at this store."

When he said this, I totally lost it and, once more, began laughing hysterically. I gasped, "He . . . he must wonder about our diet!"

"The guy probably thinks we're nuts! Can't you . . . can't you just hear him telling his family about us over dinner?" And so we laughed some more . . . and more . . . and more. My sides hurt, and yet I couldn't stop—nor did I want to. For the first time since Paul had come to our home, we were communicating—sharing a feeling. They say laughter is contagious, and it's true. People going in and out of the stores smiled at us; some even laughed as if they knew what was so funny. As an elderly, stern-looking woman approached the entrance to Phar-Mor, Paul said, "Wonder why she's going in there? They don't even have a cheese cooler."

She apparently heard what he said because, as she entered the store, she gave him a strange look. Of course, that only made us laugh all the more. We must have appeared ridiculous—two supposedly mature adults, acting like teenagers.

Finally, we got into the car, chatting and cutting up the whole time. We drove to the right store and exchanged the ricotta. This time we encountered no problems, and our light-hearted attitude prevailed all the way home. Yes, the ice had been broken between us, but there would be many more storms ahead.

✦ 6 ✦

The Friend with Many Faces

*Though good advice lies deep within a counselor's heart, the
wise man will draw it out.*

Proverbs 20:5

The week following the cheese caper, we received a letter sloppily addressed to "The Sterlings." I ripped open the envelope and found a sheet of lined notebook paper with a short message written in unfamiliar handwriting. It read: "If someone molested *your* child, would you be so willing to help him? He belongs in jail, not in your house."

Next it was a telephone call from a woman who mumbled something about all of us belonging in jail. About a week later, there was a second, similar call, and then the harassment stopped.

Doug and I were puzzled by these incidents because only a few trusted friends were aware that Paul was staying with us. Then we remembered! One evening, about a week before receiving the letter, Doug had taken Paul to see someone who lived about forty miles north of our city. On the way they stopped at a restaurant for coffee and, unexpectedly, ran into a young man from our former church. After a brief exchange of conversation, they went their separate ways. It had to be from this chance meeting that the word had been spread. Doug and I decided not to tell Paul or his wife about the letter or phone calls, because we knew he would insist on leaving. He was insecure enough already—always expecting something to go wrong, always wondering when we might ask him to leave.

Every time he returned from one of his twelve-step meetings for sex addicts, he would ask, "What's wrong? You guys seem so quiet." Also, whenever he phoned, he would question us, "Is everything okay? Your voice sounds funny."

Another thing that puzzled us was that, although Paul's work was excellent, he never completed one job before beginning another. There would be one tree not trimmed, one section of the house not painted, two tiles not replaced in the bathroom. Later, I came to realize that this was his subconscious method of keeping people from commenting about his work. If he never finished the work, no one could compliment him on doing a good job. Also, no one could hurt him by saying he had done a bad job. He was attempting to control people, to protect himself from the pain of rejection or from the compliments he didn't believe he was worthy to receive. As time passed, we witnessed more and more obsessive behavior in his desire to control and manipulate people, situations, and events.

Paul and Marie were blessed to have a Christian counseling center less than twenty miles from their home that specialized in treating sexual disorders. Bill, the founder of the center, continued to be a tremendous help to their entire family. I honestly believe that if it weren't for his wise Christian counseling, their marriage probably would have ended, and Paul wouldn't have been able to start down the road to recovery. As a qualified therapist, Bill pulled no punches regarding the severity of the charges, and he worked with the court system to provide the best treatment possible for Paul. Early in the treatment program, Bill arranged for Paul to enter a RAPHA Christian Psychiatric Hospital in San Antonio, Texas. The word *rapha* comes from the Old Testament. It is one of the names of God—*Jehovah Rapha* means "God the Healer." Upon Paul's return, he saw Bill every week for individual and group counseling. Bill also contacted the leader of a twelve-step program for people suffering from sexual addiction and made arrangements for Paul to attend their meetings.

One of Bill's assistants was counseling Marie on a regular basis, getting her through one day at a time. Her work situation had deteriorated to the point where it was almost intolerable. People would whisper, judge, speculate, and ignore her. They hated her husband for what he had done, and since she was his wife and hadn't left him, they were angry with her. To their way of thinking, his guilt was her guilt, and deep inside, I believe Marie struggled with those same thoughts. *Had there been warning signs? How could she have lived with this man for so long and not noticed something?* The opinions of other people were having a direct effect on their marriage. Over and over she heard, "After what he's done, how can you possibly stay with him?" So far, I had refrained from expressing any opinion about this to her.

"I don't think I can stay with him," she would say. "Ann and I can get along by ourselves." But then the next day it would be, "We vowed to be together in sickness and health—and he's sick." She frequently changed her mind, sometimes expressing her anger toward him and other times attempting to comprehend what he had done and why. Intellectually she was forced to accept what was disclosed to her about her husband's actions, but inwardly she remained in denial of the facts.

Our home became a weekend refuge for Marie. Sometimes during her visits, she would ignore Paul; other times they would exchange critical, hurting words. Occasionally they would hold hands, even give each other a good-bye hug before she left for home. She was a woman influenced by the past, living the pain of the present, and afraid to trust in the future. *Both of them are so hurt and depressed they could be suicidal,* I thought. *God, why did you allow us to become so involved in their lives? Why did you bring this sex offender to live in our home?*

Since our laughter and sharing at Phar-Mor, Paul and I became more comfortable with one another. Conversation during lunch and afternoon tea breaks became easier. Paul even began to share general information with Doug and me about his twelve-step program for sexual addiction. He said that the leaders of the program had assured him that his anonymity would be protected. He seemed appreciative of the fellowship, support, and understanding that he received at these meetings. The members came from all walks of life, and being able to share similar problems with them was helpful. As his arraignment date grew closer, these people, who barely knew him, began to express concern and offer prayers on his behalf. Some had been in the program for years; others, like Paul, were fairly new. Doug and I listened politely, knowing that he needed someone to talk with. Also, deep within me was a need to understand the reasons for the sexual behavior that had led to his arrest.

One afternoon Paul was unusually quiet as we ate lunch. "Is something wrong?" I asked.

"Nothing more than usual. When I called Marie last night, I realized that it's getting more and more difficult for her to continue working. And yet, she needs to work—to fill her hours—to stay busy."

"Not if her job is destroying her."

"Her job's not destroying her; I am . . . I'm the pervert who destroyed her life."

I was startled by the emotion in his voice and didn't know how to reply, so I remained silent. He continued talking. "Beth, I knew a person who wanted to share something personal but couldn't because the information could be incriminating. So what that person did was to talk about a friend instead." He paused. "I . . . I want to talk to you about my friend."

Nervously, without thinking, I began twisting a strand of my short blond hair around my fingers. "I understand," I said.

"Well, my friend was doing things he hated—it seemed no matter how hard he tried, he couldn't stop. He would really try, but he just couldn't help himself. He said the things he did felt good while he was doing them, but afterwards he would be sick with shame, guilt, and self-disgust. He began to take more and more chances. I believe in the end that he deliberately set himself up so that he would get caught."

"How could you—I mean he—do that?"

"He'd been making phone calls—improper ones—when he read in his newspaper that the calls were being investigated. Not only did he continue to make the calls, but he intentionally began calling the same people over and over, making it easier for the calls to be traced."

"And so he got caught."

"Yes—but his family is suffering. They'd probably be better off if he were dead—they could start their lives over!"

I gave him a searching look. "Is that what your friend really wants?"

"No," he said, his voice choking. "What he wants is to be with his family!"

The conversation about his imaginary friend ended, but he would surface again in later conversations, usually in connection with guilt, fear of prison, or worry for his family.

Although I tried my best to be kind and offer Paul support, it was difficult.

Many times Doug and I witnessed Paul's explosive temper. His sudden outbursts of anger were sometimes exaggerated, usually inappropriate, and easily triggered. Once, the three of us had gone to a restaurant for dinner. When Paul found out that the salad bar had run out of chili, he instantly became furious. First he vented his anger toward the waitress, then directed it toward the manager. Based on his actions, one would have thought he had intentionally been singled out to be deprived of his chili. Later, after calming down, he apologized to Doug and me and became very subdued. He told us he didn't understand his anger or why he behaved that way.

Paul could also be the ultimate charmer, calling a waitress by name, getting a smile from even the gloomiest of faces. In his dealings with people, I felt he could talk a person into anything when it was in his best interest. This ability, undoubtedly, was one of the main reasons why he was able to conduct telephone sex surveys with such expertise. I shuddered, wondering how many people he had conned—and in what ways. Although this was his first arrest, it probably only meant that he hadn't been caught before. Somehow, from what I had read in the newspaper, I had doubts that his inappropriate sexual behavior had developed overnight. He was definitely a man with many problems.

It didn't take long for me to realize that Paul was extremely intelligent; his vocabulary was amazing. Perhaps this was partly attributable to study habits he developed as a lonely youngster when he enjoyed reading books such as the encyclopedia and dictionary. Whenever I encountered a problem with a word used by an author in a manuscript, Paul became my walking reference book. I found that he usually knew not only the meaning, but also the correct spelling.

His knowledge of the Bible also surprised me. One evening I was studying a college course in Old Testament history. To test me, my daughter asked questions from the study guide. Paul was in the room with us, and whenever I had difficulty with a question, he couldn't seem to resist giving the answer. I couldn't understand why he hadn't been able to use Christian principles, which he knew so well, in the way he lived his own life.

· 7 ·

Filthy Rags

We are all infected and impure with sin. When we put on our prized robes of righteousness we find they are but filthy rags. Like autumn leaves we fade, wither and fall. And our sins, like the wind, sweep us away.

Isaiah 64:6

It was early in the evening. Doug, Paul, and I had gone outside to sit on the patio, seeking relief from the hot, humid August weather.

"It's miserable in the house," Doug said. "I think I'll sleep out here tonight. How about you Beth—care to join me?"

"Not me; you know how I hate bugs. I'd rather we get air-conditioning!"

Just then Tina came out of the house. "Paul," she said, "your wife's on the phone—she wants to talk to you." As Paul got up to go inside, Tina walked toward her car. "Bye, Mom! Bye, Dad! I'm going over to pick up Abby and go to a movie. See you later!"

Doug and I sat waiting for Paul to return. It was too early for him to have gone to bed, and besides, he never retired without saying good-night to us. But, apparently, tonight was to be the exception. *Bad news*, I thought. *He and Marie must have had a disagreement.*

The next morning I awoke at 7:30 and, after dressing, hurried to the kitchen to fix breakfast. The door to Paul's room was closed, which struck me as unusual since he was normally out of bed and working by this time. Sipping my orange juice, I shrugged off the feeling of uneasiness that had begun to interfere with my work plans for the day. My desk was piled high with correspondence waiting to be answered, but I didn't go down to my office. Instead, I cleaned the kitchen, waiting for Paul to get out of bed. By 10:00 A.M., I felt that something had to be wrong but didn't know what to do. The word *suicide* subtly entered my mind, then intensified with each passing moment. "He wouldn't do something that dumb," I murmured to myself. "Not now, after all this time."

It was now 10:30 A.M. My uneasiness and fears wouldn't allow me to wait any longer—I had to check on him. Apprehensively, I knocked lightly on his door. No answer! I knocked a little louder this time, while calling out, "Paul, are you okay?"

After a moment he answered, "Yes, I'm fine; I'll be out as soon as I get dressed."

I was relieved that apparently he was okay. However, his voice sounded tired and listless.

When he came to the kitchen, I handed him a cup of tea. "You look as though you could use this, but be careful; it's hot."

He didn't say anything as he walked over and sat down at the breakfast bar. He drank the hot tea quickly, acting as though his mouth and throat didn't feel the heat. Something was weighing heavily on his mind.

"Can I fix you some breakfast?" I asked. "I know you normally don't eat first thing in the morning, but today you're up later than usual."

"No thanks, Beth; I'm not hungry."

"Well then, I guess I'll go down to my office. I'll fix you a sandwich later on. Let me know when you're hungry." I started to leave when he softly spoke—so softly that I had to ask him to repeat himself.

"Beth, I don't know what to do. I've hurt my family more than . . . more than . . ." He stopped, unable to find the right words. Then he continued. "Marie was crying when she called last night. She had an especially bad day with her coworkers. In addition to what they've been saying to her, she's received some anonymous, harassing phone calls at home."

"But that isn't anything new. It's been happening ever since your arrest."

"Yesterday wasn't the same; it was worse! Remember the hearing I went to day before yesterday? Well, there was a write-up in the newspaper about it—a terrible write-up."

"How detailed was it?" I asked, sitting down across from him.

"When Marie read it to me, it sounded like the résumé of a sex pervert. And now, once again she's feeling the shame and humiliation of being married to me. It's not fair to her."

I sighed. "No, it isn't, but as Doug says, 'You can't unscramble an egg.'"

"Maybe not, but I can get an unlisted phone number. I don't know why I didn't think of getting one before now."

"You've had other things on your mind. And, eventually, so will the people who are harassing your wife."

"Sure! Until the next news release. It won't stop until I've been in jail long enough for them to forget. Forget me; maybe! Forgive me; never!"

"God forgives."

He stood up and spoke with sarcasm and anger. "Does he really? Well, I'm pleased to know that he can forgive me for something that, despite my pleas, he hasn't taken away from me—my compulsive, sick, sexual desires. I have begged, cried, and tried to bargain with him, but nothing has ever changed." Suddenly he looked up and cried aloud, "You! God! Why don't you hear me? Why don't you answer me? I'm messed up, really messed up! Don't you care?"

Am I witnessing the performance of a master con artist, trying to get sympathy? I asked myself. *Or is he being sincere?*

I chose my words carefully. "God does hear you. Your desire to get caught—how do you know that didn't come from him? And what about your Christian counselor and your support groups? Isn't it possible that they could be God's answer to your pleas for help? And how about all your friends?"

He sat down and verbally challenged me. "Yes," he replied sarcastically. "There are my many friends! Tell me, Beth, when I go to jail, how often will you and Doug come to visit your friend? Just how easy has it been for you to forgive? When you see me and talk to me, what do you think I am—bad, mad, or sick?"

"I know you're sick," I said. But that was as far as I could go.

He stared at his empty cup for a moment, then, pushing it aside, he arose and went outside.

A few days later, while putting a load of clothes into the washing machine, I noticed the condition of one of Doug's shirts. He must have worn it while working on the car. I had always liked this particular shirt, but now it appeared to be ruined. It was covered with grease and ground-in dirt. It was absolutely filthy. *This is hopeless*, I thought. *I might as well burn it in our potbellied stove.*

Walking over to the furnace area where the stove was located, I opened the door and was about to throw the shirt in the fire. Suddenly, I heard a voice saying, "Stop!" No, it wasn't Doug; although if he had been home, that's exactly what he would have said. It was a voice from deep within my spirit—a voice that was also reminding me of Isaiah 64:6: "We are all infected and impure with sin. When we put on our prized robes of righteousness we find they are but filthy rags. Like autumn leaves we fade, wither and fall. And our sins, like the wind, sweep us away." I didn't throw the shirt away; instead, I went to my office, sat down, and began to meditate. *What are you telling me, God?*

According to Webster's dictionary, the word *filthy* means covered with filth, offensively dirty, foul matter, loathsome dirt or refuse, and obscene. However, the Bible says that a person's righteousness is as filthy rags. I can't think of a stronger word than *filthy* to describe something dirty. And yet, we are *all* filthy without Christ's righteousness. God doesn't say that murderers are dirty, adulterers are stained, liars are soiled, and gossipers are slightly tinged. Nor does he say that only those with a sexual addiction are filthy! God puts all of us in the same sin category. If we profess religion instead of Jesus, we are like the autumn leaves, which fade, grow dry, wither, and fall. Some blow away while others are raked and burned.

I didn't burn Doug's shirt. Instead, I used spot remover, soaked it in strong prewash, and ran it through the heavy-duty cycle of my washing machine. When it was finished, I was pleased with how it looked, realizing that God must also feel this way about his children after they have been washed clean by his son, Jesus.

Washed, I thought. *It sounds so simple. Just forgive and forget. But God, I'm not you! I'm human and feel so torn.* It was as if my spirit and mind were in conflict and pulling me in opposite directions.

Angrily, I said aloud, "You don't understand, God. You just don't understand. I was just a child. Only eleven! I had been taught to trust all adults. They were supposed to take care of me—make me feel safe and secure. Not only my parents, but all adults: teachers, ministers, doctors, mechanics, mailmen, policemen, firemen—everybody. They were supposed to be there for me . . . to make the world a safe place. After Mr. Stephens betrayed that trust by molesting me, nothing was ever the same again. I was frightened and felt different than other kids. I no longer trusted adults."

Any moment I expected to hear God's voice shouting a reply—but there was only silence. I thought about how he relates to his children. *Why hadn't he protected me? Why hadn't one of the adults I trusted so much protected me?* Every child's sexuality is a gift from God and should be allowed to develop naturally, being expressed and enjoyed in a loving way at the right time of his or her life. No child needs an adult to inappropriately teach him or her about sex. Even when there is no physical force involved in the molestation, the child is still being manipulated and coerced by the adult.

Many people, even strong Christians, have a great deal of difficulty dealing with the sexual molesting of children. And yet this crime, which is so prevalent in today's society, has been an ongoing problem for generations. Within my own life, there have been several examples: my mother and the minister, Mr. Stephens and my friend Janice, Mr. Stephens and me, the neighbor who attended my childhood church, and now Paul.

God, I thought. *What causes a man or woman to victimize a child? How can these offenders be helped—these offenses stopped? Can I learn to judge the sin and not the sinner? Can I use my anger to bring about change, not just to condemn? Will I ever be able to truthfully and totally confront my past and learn to forgive? Lord, I know what you tell us about forgiving, but it's so hard to do.*

I realized that, in some ways, I was just like Paul—unable to apply all of God's truths in my life.

8

Tears and Forgiveness

*And we know that all that happens to us
is working for our good if we love God and are fitting into
his plans.*

Romans 8:28

God used a thirty-minute television special to help
open doors in our relationship with Paul. When
Doug realized that the program was about child
molestation, he got up from his chair to change
the channel.

"No," Paul said, "you don't have to change the program
because of me."

But I thought Doug was right; we'd all be too uncomfortable. "Paul, there are other programs we can watch."

However he was insistent. "Watch what you want—I've disrupted your lives enough."

"Changing the channel isn't a big deal," Doug said, going back to his chair. "I just didn't think this program would be very relaxing for you."

"I don't know how to relax," he said. "But the program won't bother me—it's reality."

He was wrong! It did bother him; it bothered all of us! The story was about an eight-year-old girl who had been sexually molested in a violent way by her neighbor. Even though she suffered physical injury, it was the emotional scars that her parents were the most concerned about. The little girl looked like a frightened animal as she clung to her mother. Her parents described how she would wake up screaming because of nightmares. To reassure her, they had to leave lights on so she could see that no one was lurking in the darkness. Sometimes, when her father came near her, she would scream and run away. Other times she would cling to him and sob in his arms.

With tears in their eyes, the outraged parents spoke of their daughter's ordeal. They stated, "If we could get our hands on the guy who did this to our little girl, we'd kill him. He robbed her of her innocence and ability to trust." When the parents began to cry, I wanted to cry with them. Instead, I clenched my hands so tightly that my fingernails cut into my palms.

When the program ended, our mood was somber. Doug turned off the TV, and without discussing the program, we said good-night to one another and went to our rooms.

All night, in my dreams, I saw filthy rags swirling above a merry-go-round filled with children. The merry-go-round moved slowly, but somehow I knew that it was never going to stop—that the sad children riding it would never get off. Over and over I tried to climb onto the merry-go-round so I could reach the children, but every time, rags descended upon me, blinding me, and smothering my attempts. Finally I cried out the name of Jesus, and the rags turned into white clouds that floated down, enveloped the children, and carried them away. The clouds were beautiful, and I felt wonderfully happy—that is until I saw a new group of children on the merry-go-round. It had never stopped moving and was again being guarded by filthy rags! "No!" I screamed. "Stop!"

I roused myself sufficiently to pull myself into a sitting position. There I sat, awake, until daybreak. Although physically and emotionally exhausted, I was anxious to get out of bed and away from my dream—anxious to begin a new day in my office.

Around 9:00 A.M. I gave my secretary some correspondence to type and went upstairs. Paul was in the kitchen eating a bowl of cereal. He commented on my appearance.

"Beth, you look tired. Didn't you sleep well?"

"No. Something was on my mind!"

He was forthright. "It was the show we watched, wasn't it?"

Looking at him accusingly I said, "Yes, it bothered me. I was angry! I don't understand how a person could be so messed up that they could hurt a child that way!"

"There are many men and women in the world who are sexually out of control—doing things they don't want to do—unable to stop!"

"Are you saying they can't stop? That's hard for me to believe!"

"I'm not exaggerating, Beth. Addicts don't have a choice. In that particular area of their lives they've totally lost control, and even though they try, they find that they can't stop. All of us have heard about someone who is addicted to chocolate; or a better example is the alcoholic who can't take even one drink of alcohol without losing control and wanting more and more. Well, for a sex addict, any lustful sexual activity has exactly the same effect as a drink does on an alcoholic. One drink—one lustful incident—leads to another in a progressively addictive and destructive pattern, and before long, the person is hooked and unable to stop. Usually addicts must hit their own personal bottom, realizing that they want to stop but can't, before they will seek out the people and recovery programs that God has provided for them."

Bitterly, I asked, "But, until that time, who protects the children? Who protected your victims?"

He knew better than to try to respond. Instead he continued to speak in generalities. "Beth, it's . . . it's so complicated. Most people suffering from sexual addiction feel that their love, acceptance, self-worth, and even their very survival as a person depends on their sexual performance. For a sex addict, loving relationships don't exist—only sexual ones."

"That's still no excuse for hurting others—especially children!"

"It usually isn't like what we saw on TV last night. Most molesters don't use physical force, they stop if the child resists in any way."

"Of course they do. They don't want to get caught! They know if they don't stop, the child will probably tell on them."

"You're right. They don't want to go to jail. That's why only a small percent use physical violence. But there's something else, too. According to what I've been reading, a child molester has an uncanny ability to sense which child is most likely *not* to resist. He seems to know which child is available."

I didn't like what he was saying. "What do you mean by 'available'?"

"Children who, for any reason, are hurting. For example, there is the lonely child who doesn't fit in and is looking for love and acceptance. He or she is starved for affection and will do anything to get it, including the trading of sex to fill an emotional need. And then there are those who have suffered previous physical, emotional, or sexual abuse." He paused momentarily. "Some children come from well-adjusted homes and have no obvious need, but they still get molested. It doesn't matter what the cause is; these are children who have had their trust betrayed by an adult."

I shivered. "The way you put it, it sounds as though the child molester is like the big bad wolf, trying to grab Little Red Riding Hood."

"That's not how they see themselves; they believe they're filling a need. In my case, I was so out of touch with reality that I began to believe that everyone was available to me regardless of age. I was so sick that I didn't use my inner or common sense—I just reached out."

"And you got caught."

"Yes, Beth, I got caught. But, unfortunately, most offenders never do."

He's saying all the right things, I thought, *but is he just speaking words or is he speaking from his heart?* Aloud, I asked, "Why not?"

"There are many reasons. Sometimes, parents don't report it because of the publicity. Or, they may not want their child to face the offender in court. Or, the offender may be a close friend or relative."

"I personally think parents feel ashamed and guilty because they didn't protect their child. And so they keep quiet."

"Beth, would you believe that some parents don't report it because their child willingly participated in the abuse for a long period of time?"

"Willingly participated," I echoed, my eyes narrowing. "That's pure garbage! No child willingly wants to be abused! Anyone who says so is just trying to justify their actions."

He looked upset. "Just read the psychiatric case histories of those who molest children, and you'll find that what I'm saying is true!" He paused, choosing his next words carefully. "Sometimes . . . sometimes it's the child who initiates the sexual contact."

I was furious. "If that's true, I doubt if it is sex they're looking for. I also doubt that they're trying to take advantage of a poor, helpless adult. Come on, Paul, get real! Can you tell me how these learned psychiatrists—these great experts— define *willingly participating?*" My voice became tense and louder; I was losing control. "If a girl doesn't scream, does that mean she's willingly participating? Maybe she's too scared to scream or say no—or too embarrassed—or in shock—or maybe just doesn't know what to say or do!"

"Beth, calm down! You're getting so loud your whole staff will hear you."

"I don't care if they do. I'm upset! What is a child to do if the abuser is a respected adult? Perhaps an uncle, brother, cousin, grandfather, or even a parent?"

"The child should tell," Paul said, "no matter who the offender is. The list is endless. It could be a close friend of the parents, a person from the church, a teacher at school, a . . ."

When Paul said, "friend of the parents," the emotions from my childhood experience overwhelmed me, and I heard nothing more. Abruptly I stood up and began to pace back and forth across the kitchen floor. My head was pounding from lack of sleep; my emotions were taut. "A friend of the parents," I murmured, ". . . my parents . . . someone like Mr. Stephens!"

"Who? . . . What did you say?" Paul asked, as he stood and took my arm to stop me from pacing. "Beth, what are you talking about? You're not making sense!"

"What happened to me when I was eleven didn't make sense either." My eyes looked into his. "That's when Mr. Stephens, my next-door neighbor, molested me."

He turned pale and immediately stepped back to put distance between us. Hoarsely he whispered, "I'm sorry! So sorry!"

By now I was sobbing. "Did you tell *them* you were sorry? Oh, Paul, do you know how easy it would be for me to hate you?"

"Go ahead. Everyone else does. And I don't blame them—I hate myself! You have no idea how many times I've begged God to forgive me. How many prayers I've prayed. How many times I've turned to the Bible. How many promises I've made. But, no matter what I did, the sexual fantasies and compulsive desires that drove me didn't leave. Try to understand," he pleaded, "that I don't want to be the way I am!"

"And I don't believe that any child wants to be molested!"

"Anyone who molests a child, including your Mr. Stephens, needs help. Sexual addiction is a progressive illness. That's why I *had* to get caught."

It was his face, not his words, which finally convinced me that he was telling the truth. The best con artist couldn't fake the raw emotions that were reflected on his face. *God,* I prayed silently, *he needs you—help him! And help me, too!*

In my spirit, I heard God whisper, "Learn to forgive—help one another!"

As we again sat down, I forced my voice to sound softer. "Paul," I said, "I don't hate you. It's just that I . . . I haven't been able to handle my mixed-up emotions."

"Beth, if I'd known that you had been molested, I never would have asked to stay here. But, thank God, you and Doug were here for me when others turned away. Not that I blame them for feeling the way they do. I know I wouldn't want an accused child molester near my daughter!"

When I didn't respond, he continued, "Believe it or not, I was despised and hated the most while I was in jail. When the other prisoners found out that I was an accused child molester, they threatened to kill me and harm my family. They respect murderers, bank robbers, and drug dealers but have only contempt for a child molester. I lived in constant fear of being attacked. It became so bad that I was even afraid to go to sleep, so I tore off pieces of my toenails to cause pain severe enough to keep me awake."

I gasped. "What a horrible experience!"

"Horrible doesn't even begin to describe it. I'll kill myself before I go back there!"

He means it, I thought. *He would kill himself*. Aloud, I said, "If you do something dumb like that, you'll be deserting your wife and little girl. Is that what you want?"

"I wouldn't be deserting them; I'd be setting them free," he argued. "And besides, it's cheaper than a divorce."

"Not in terms of pain. They'd feel abandoned."

"Abandoned," he repeated softly as he walked into our living room and slumped wearily onto the easy chair. I returned to my office, emotionally drained, but knowing that more needed to be said.

I found it hard to concentrate on work and was glad when the day finally ended and my staff left. Now I could relax and enjoy a quiet dinner and evening with my husband. But it was not to be!

After dinner, Paul brought up the word *abandonment* again. "I hate that word," he said. "It reminds me of stray puppies, kittens—and little boys."

"Little boys?" Doug asked.

"Yes! When my parents got divorced, that's how it felt— like I was abandoned and didn't belong to anyone anymore— like I didn't have a home."

"Did you live with your mom?" I asked.

"No, not at that time. Initially the courts gave my grandparents custody. I can clearly remember," he said, closing his eyes, "how hard I cried when the judge asked me which parent I wanted to live with."

"How old were you?"

"Four."

"That's really young to be separated from your mom and dad."

"I could visit with my mom; she lived near my grandparents. And my dad came to see me a few days each year."

"Paul," Doug said, "you weren't abandoned! You had people who cared for you."

His reply was sarcastic. "*People* is the right word. Various people. When I was almost eight, my mom moved to Ohio to work and, just like my dad, she only came to see me a few days each year. Then, when I was twelve, she returned with her new husband. At that point in my life I was such an angry, rebellious child that my grandparents said they couldn't cope with me any longer on a full-time basis. Once again I felt abandoned, unloved, and unwanted. Another message of rejection to me that said I was no good."

"Where did you go then?" Doug asked.

"First I went to live with my mom and stepdad. It was my hope that I would now have a normal home with a mom and dad—not grandparents. I thought if I had parents, perhaps I wouldn't feel so different from the other kids!"

Doug questioned him. "Did it work out?"

"No, not really. It didn't take long for me to find out that my new home was far from normal. Things are never normal in a home where alcohol is god. Most days I'd fix my own breakfast, go to school, then go to work setting pins in a bowling alley until 11:00 P.M."

Surprisingly, Doug, who never talks much about personal matters, volunteered information about himself. "I know how alcohol can affect a family. For a few years my mom had a drinking problem, and we went through some bad times."

"Then you know what I mean. I had to work if I wanted clothes for school. Many times I wouldn't have had anything to eat if it weren't for the money I earned. My stepdad was a dreamer who was always going to make a million dollars—tomorrow. Every day he had a new get-rich-quick scheme. But the reality was that he drove a taxi all night long, and we were always poor."

"I didn't go through anything like that," Doug said. "My dad was a good provider, but he and my mom would argue when she was drinking. I used to cry because I didn't understand why they were fighting."

"At my mother's house, weekends were the worst," Paul said. "That's when Mom and my stepdad drank and fought the most. They never paid any attention to me or what I did. Sometimes when my mom was drunk, she'd bring a man home with her from the bar. At first, seeing and hearing them together in the bedroom would bother me, but when you grow up in an alcoholic home, you soon become numb and learn to deny your feelings. In order to survive, I learned to bury my feelings about their behavior and our way of living. My pain was real on the inside, but I refused to let it show on the outside."

Seeing that Doug didn't know how to respond, I changed the subject and asked Paul about his father. "Did your dad remarry?"

Once again, he replied with sarcasm. "Yeah, he remarried, and we became one big happy family. He and my new stepmom, who was only four years older than me, rented an apartment on the other side of town. They became close friends with my mom and stepdad. Often, the four of them would get together for the weekend to play cards and drink beer. Then, on Sunday, my dad and stepmom would go home to sober up for work the next day. Sometimes, when I saw all of them together, my feelings and emotions would become so mixed up and confused that, just to get away from them, I would leave the house for the entire weekend. When I returned home, never once did they ask where I had been. It was like I was never missed—I was the invisible kid—no one cared if I even existed!"

Doug questioned him, "If living with your mom was so bad, why didn't you move in with your dad?"

"I did. When I was a teenager I moved in with him and my stepmom a couple of times."

"What happened?"

"It never worked out. He didn't understand me, and I didn't understand him; we were strangers to one another. Besides, my stepmom was too close to my age, and we fought all the time. I was like a nomad, moving from house to house. It seemed to be a great way of life for me—I could pick and choose where I wanted to live—whatever suited my purposes at the time. Summers were the best," he said, thoughtfully, "because I enjoyed staying with my grandparents in the country. If you're an invisible kid, no one cares when you move in or out."

My questions grew more and more personal, yet I felt compelled to ask them. I also knew that Paul wanted and needed to talk. "You're saying you were never close to either of your parents?"

"Beth, I don't know what the word *close* means! Maybe you can tell me."

"Did your parents ever say they loved you? Were there hugs and kisses? Touching?"

"Oh, I had lots of hugs, kisses, and touches; but none come from my parents. I discovered girls . . . or maybe I should say they discovered me, at an early age." I could tell by the flatness of his voice that he wasn't bragging.

Doug interjected, "Paul, I believe she's talking about nurturing—not romance."

"I'm not sure I know the difference between the two. When I was about eight, visiting with my mom, there were two neighbor girls—sisters—twelve and thirteen, who taught and showed me everything there was to know about sex. I'm not exaggerating or talking about kids' games. It was everything!"

Doug gasped. "Are you telling us that they molested you?"

"That's exactly what I'm saying. They took turns doing it with me for almost a year, for hours at a time, over and over, almost every day, until my mom moved to Ohio. While our moms talked upstairs, the girls and I would be playing our secret games down in the basement. I got rewarded, too, with cookies, sugar bread, candy, or whatever they wanted to give me."

My head was spinning—trying to comprehend what he was saying. "Why didn't you tell on them? Were you afraid your mother wouldn't believe you?"

"Do you want the truth?"

"Of course we do!"

"I didn't tell because I thoroughly enjoyed what they were doing. Finally, someone was paying attention to me: touching me, holding me, doing things with me that made me feel loved and wanted. I was important to them. They didn't know it, but they were feeding a love-starved child. And I was pleasing them—giving them pleasure in return. Later, when I was older, I came to realize that through sex they gave me a feeling of acceptance."

I fought back tears as Doug said, "Paul, they used you—exploited you—for their own selfish purposes! You should be angry—hate them!"

"Bill at the counseling center doesn't agree with you. He tells me I should hate what they did but not hate them. The truth is I don't hate them or what they did to me, so how can I make myself feel something that isn't there? It's either there or it isn't."

"And you never told anyone about the girls?"

"Not until I was arrested and started in counseling. I told Bill, Marie, and now I've told you two!"

"When your mother moved, did you continue to see the girls?" I asked.

"No. But there were many others willing to replace them—the difference being that I was now usually the initiator. Playing doctor, house, and marriage with girls my age, or a little older or younger, became my main focus in life. And all my new partners thought the games we played were great—that it was exciting to share in the secret. As we grew older, the games became more elaborate and more fun. The more sexual experience I gained, the more my self-confidence seemed to grow. Being accepted as a person of worth somehow became related to the number of girls who said yes to me. In retrospect, I now wish that some had said no instead of being so eager to participate."

Trying to put this into perspective was difficult for me, and judging by Doug's next comment, also for him. "But Paul, I'm confused. Are you sexually attracted to children or adults? Your arrest involved young girls, and yet you have a wife and children."

"Bill told me that because I'm also sexual with adult women, I'm not a fixated pedophile. In fact, for years I've had problems trying to control my attraction to women, both before and after marriage. When I got married, because I was so much in love, I sincerely believed that my feelings for my wife and the sexual fulfillment of the wedding bed would curb my compulsive sexual behavior—but it didn't. I now know that there is no quick-fix cure for sexual addiction. Through my counseling and Sexaholics Anonymous meetings, I'm learning how to cope with it one day at a time. Jesus, who is my higher power, helps me to get through every one of those days."

"It's too bad you didn't get counseling years ago."

"Doug, even if I had known that it was available, because of the depth of my shame and guilt, I doubt that I would have gone for the help."

"Why not? It could have changed your entire life."

"Because I believed that, under the child protection laws, the counselor would have to report me to the police. And to be honest, after a while I became such an expert at conning others that it became easy to con myself. I became convinced that because so many other people were doing it, it was okay for me to do it, too. I now know that it was irrational thinking, but at the time I really believed it."

"Did you also con Marie?" I asked.

"No. I never gave her any reason to suspect me. I've always been a loving husband and responsible father, providing for the needs of my family. She had no idea that I was wearing a

mask most of the time—trying to hide and control my obsessive, destructive sexual desire from her.

"All my life I've been confessing, repenting, and falling . . .
confessing, repenting, and falling . . . confessing, repenting,
and falling. Over and over again I went through the motions,
but I believed my sins were too great and too many for God
to forgive. Sometimes I still feel that way, even though I know
what his Word says."

I tried to encourage him. "Paul, you'll have to allow the
Word to grow strong enough in you so that you can over-
power all those doubts you have."

Doug stood up and extended his hand toward Paul in a ges-
ture of friendship, saying, "Paul, you have a great deal of good
in you. There's so much about you that we respect. Beth and
I truly want to be your friends; we want to be real with you."

Before taking Doug's hand, Paul brushed away the tears
that had begun to roll down his cheeks. "What is real? I don't
know if there is a real me, or even what reality is."

"Deep down inside, there's a real you just waiting to break
free. I'm sure your Christian counselor and psychologist can
help you find that invisible kid. Perhaps, one day, you'll be
able to help others who have your problem."

"*Problems*," he emphasized. "I have more than one."

"Problem—problems," I said. "Who cares if you have one
or fifty? The main thing is that something good can come out
of any problem if you're open to God. You know, you've
helped me realize that I haven't totally forgiven the man who
molested me. If I can do that, maybe then I'll finally be free
of all this guilt . . ."

"What guilt?" Paul interrupted. "You didn't do anything
wrong."

"But I did! If I had been more forceful in telling on him,
my parents would have reported him and then . . . then . . .
maybe he wouldn't have been free to sexually force himself
on a high school girl years later. I was married when he was

finally arrested. I felt terrible for the girl . . . and I keep wondering how many other victims there were between my experience and hers."

"Beth," Paul said, his voice firm but kind. "It's not your fault. Stop blaming yourself; you were only a child. And remember, if he used physical force, it was unusual—most pedophiles aren't violent."

"I know what you're saying is true. Paul, I can see that you aren't like he was, but when I look at you, I see glimpses of him in you. And when I remember how he was, I see glimpses of you in him. I need to see Christ—to forgive. By forgiving you I feel that, somehow, I'll also be forgiving him—not just for what he did to me but also for making me feel guilty about his other victims. Only then can I have the peace that God intends for me to have." My voice quivered as tears came to my eyes. I felt Doug take my hand. Looking up, I noticed that he was also teary-eyed. I reached out and took Paul's hand, saying, "These tears are for you, your victims, and all the lost childhoods."

This is good, I thought. *For me, this is the beginning of total forgiveness, and for Paul, this is the start of his search for reality.*

✦ 9 ✦

Sexual Addiction—
What Is It?

For the Lord grants wisdom! His every word is a treasure
of knowledge and understanding.

Proverbs 2:6

Many of us have left our doctor's office only to go home and look up the diagnosis in a medical reference book because we didn't understand the medical terms. Yes, we had asked the doctor questions, but not satisfied with the answers, we sought more detailed information about our condition. There is a strong need within each of us to fully understand things. The unknown frightens us.

In order to learn about sexual addiction and write a book about it, I knew it was essential to begin with an accurate definition. Most experts agree that sexual addiction is a pathological relationship in which obsessive/compulsive sexual behavior replaces a healthy relationship with a person. Not all sex addicts are sex offenders, nor are all sex offenders necessarily sex addicts. An addict is a person who is out of control; a person who cannot do without a fix. Sex addicts are preoccupied with sex; their eyes are nonstop sexual scanners, always searching for a possible connection.

To understand why sex addicts do the things they do, a person should begin by trying to comprehend the overpowering role that fantasy plays in their lives. When people are addicted to drugs or alcohol, they are using a substance to escape the pains of life. Fantasy is the substance that sex addicts use to escape similar pains. They create a different world—a fantasy world in their mind that is fortified by the reward of sexual gratification.

Over time, sex addicts' obsession with fantasy will actually reduce their ability to concentrate on even the simplest of daily tasks. They are so wrapped up in this false world that they may appear oblivious to other people. Sexual fantasy releases endorphins, chemical substances in the brain, which give them a feeling of pleasure and well-being. Endorphins cause a rush similar to the rush a person gets from eating sugar. It's not surprising that sex can easily become obsessive and addictive. Fantasies erode reality to the point where addicts can no longer accurately perceive the consequences of their actions. Reality becomes unreal—fantasy becomes reality. Not all fantasy is sexual. An addict, no matter what the addiction, can also use things like TV, radio, movies, reading, jogging, and eating to escape from reality.

Comments such as the following are frequently made by addicts:

Because I was fantasizing, I drove for three hours and couldn't even remember driving.

I was so much into fantasy that I constantly bumped into and dropped things.

Frequently my fantasies are more real to me than the actual acting out.

It seems as if I've spent my entire life in a fantasy world rather than reality.

I wonder what I could really have accomplished if I hadn't been in such a fantasy fog for most of my life.

I went to the beach and for the next three days couldn't stop fantasizing about what I had seen there.

Sunday I spent six hours watching football games, but when I was asked, I couldn't remember who played or what the scores were.

Someday I'm going to own a house of prostitution and live there forever.

Most people know very little about sexual addiction and have difficulty accepting the fact that some men and women are unable to control their sexual behavior and activity. Naturally, their hearts go out to the victims, while they judge and condemn the sex addicts or offenders. Because addicts judge themselves in the same way, they live with constant guilt, shame, pain, and fear of discovery. Since they don't trust other people, they have extreme fear and difficulty in establishing honest relationships. Until their horrible secrets become known and they receive help, they will have no peace or feelings of self-worth.

It's important to know that someone is not necessarily a sex addict just because he may have had a sexual experience that makes him feel guilty and repentant. Everyone has times in his life when his vulnerability is at a peak: during adolescence, mid-life crisis, or periods of unusual stress. In such cases, it is hoped that a lesson is learned and the same mistake not repeated. Remember, a sexually stimulated nonaddict *wants* to act out—addicts believe they *have* to act out.

Just as there are many strains of viruses, there are also many different ways in which sexual addiction may be manifested. Some examples of behavior that are tolerated, if not accepted, by society are homosexuality, prostitution, masturbation, extramarital affairs, and adult pornography (including books, magazines, photography, movies, and videotapes). When a person is involved in this type of tolerated behavior, people may say, "What they do is their own business as long as it doesn't affect me." They are wrong! It takes sick individuals to create a sick society. Sexual addiction feeds on itself. It destroys healthy relationships, is an expensive habit to support, and as it progresses (and it always does), destroys untold lives.

When it comes to voyeurism (Peeping Toms), exhibitionism (people who expose themselves in public), and indecent telephone calls, society is much less tolerant. Such behavior is abnormal and unlawful, but society tends to look at it mostly as a public nuisance. The offender is usually thought of as a disturbed and somewhat pathetic individual—a joke. However, it is no joke. The Peeping Tom or Thomasina isn't just a person who sneaks around in backyards, looking in bedroom windows, but it is someone who is constantly looking at another with lust in his heart. The flasher isn't just the cartoon caricature of a person in a raincoat, but it is someone who finds multiple ways, both covert and overt, to expose himself or herself in private and public places. The person who makes indecent phone calls isn't just a heavy breather or someone talking dirty. The calls he makes may take the form of a so-called sex survey that may sound totally legitimate. It is the real or imagined response of his victims that provides his stimulation.

Then there are the sex crimes against society which, by their very nature, are so horrible that they are unanimously condemned. These crimes—child molestation (including incest) and rape—have serious legal consequences for the person who commits them and can cause enormous long-lasting emotional and physical pain to the victim. The perpetrator of these crimes may or may not be a sex addict, but he is now a sex offender. Factors that may indicate sexual addiction include a repetitive pattern of behavior and the offender's obsession with the risk involved in the planning or committing of the crime, possibly referring to this risk-taking as a rush or high.

It is possible, in fact not unusual, for people to simultaneously experience more than one type of obsessive/compulsive addictive behavior in their lives. This is referred to as concurrent addiction. For example, an alcoholic may be a sexaholic; a sexaholic may be a workaholic; both may also be addicted to food or drugs. Because sex addicts have such low self-esteem, they may overeat in a futile attempt to mask the pain caused by their negative feelings. They then may turn to alcohol because they are, or believe they are, overweight and unattractive or because of the shame of their sexual activity. The alcohol causes lowered inhibitions, which in turn leads them into sexual activity and back to their basic problem—sexual addiction. As you can see, these addictions are interrelated and reinforce one another in a never-ending cycle.

In his book, *Out of the Shadows*, Patrick Carnes, Ph.D., describes the addictive experience as progressing through a four-step cycle, which intensifies with each repetition:

1. Preoccupation—the trance or mood wherein the addicts' minds are completely engrossed with thoughts of sex. This mental state creates an obsessive search for sexual stimulation.
2. Ritualization—the addicts' own special routines which lead up to the sexual behavior. The ritual intensifies the preoccupation, adding arousal and excitement.
3. Compulsive sexual behavior—the actual sexual act, which is the end goal of the preoccupation and ritual-

ization. Sexual addicts are unable to control or stop this behavior.
4. Despair—the feelings of utter hopelessness addicts have about their behavior and their powerlessness.[1]

When Paul discussed this cycle with his counselor, Bill told him that he believed a fifth step should be added. He called this fifth step "Denial."

It is most likely that Paul's addiction started when he was molested as a boy and then continued this learned behavior with many other children in the town. When he was eleven years old, Paul was molested again—this time by a much older boy who taught him about masturbation. In his teens and early adulthood, there was voyeurism and pornography. Later in life he became involved in extramarital affairs. Finally came the exhibitionism, child molestation, and indecent phone calls for which he was arrested.

A sex addict may have multiple sexual behavior problems. Any combination of the various types of sexual activities previously defined may be possible. For example, Paul was attracted not only to young girls but also to adult women. At the same time, he was making improper phone calls on the pretext of conducting a nationwide, sex-education survey.

As my research for this book continued, Paul read my resource books and then discussed what he had read with me in an effort to help me understand. Through these efforts, I began to understand him better, and our friendship continued to grow.

One Saturday afternoon, when Marie and Ann came to visit Paul, Marie and I did something that really upset him. She and I had gone into my bedroom to fix my hair and enjoy some woman talk. We left Paul and Doug in the living room with Ann. We were only gone about thirty minutes, but when we returned, we could tell by the look on Paul's face that he was furious. For several hours he was sullen and quiet.

When he could no longer contain his feelings, he looked at his wife angrily. "Marie," he said, "I can't believe how rude you've been!"

"What are you talking about?"

"Don't be cute," he said with bitterness in his voice. "You know very well what's bothering me. You went into the bedroom so you could talk about me! I didn't like being left alone."

I was about to reply when Marie said, "Paul, quit flattering yourself. We weren't talking about you—we were just talking. And you weren't left alone—Doug and Ann were with you!"

He became so angry that his face turned livid and the veins in his neck stood out as if they would bust. "When couples are together, they're supposed to stay together—not go off individually to whisper. What you two did was selfish and inconsiderate."

Until then, I had managed to stay out of the conversation, but when he said "you two," I just had to reply. "It wasn't selfish and inconsiderate!" I said, trying without success to keep my voice under control. "What we did is the same thing you do when you go out in the garage with Doug while he works on the car. The big difference is that when you leave us alone, we don't give a darn what you and Doug talk about."

"It's not the same—Marie knows how I feel about secrecy!"

"Then she must also know that you're paranoid about it. Doug doesn't lose any sleep worrying about what I might say about him." I looked at my husband for support.

Doug started to speak, but Paul interrupted him, "Beth, can't you understand? Doug's Doug, and I'm me—maybe he doesn't mind, but I do! If you ladies can't understand and respect how I feel about this, it might be better that Marie not come to visit. I've already got enough on my mind to deal with."

"Oh, I think I understand, all right," I said. "When your family comes to visit, your wife and I aren't allowed to be alone together."

"Not whispering together behind closed doors. I don't mind if you go shopping together, or meet for lunch—that's different."

His logic didn't make any sense, but I realized he meant every word. "Paul," I said, "regardless of how insecure you are, you can't always control the actions of other people. Eventually, you're going to have to learn to trust."

Doug, who had remained silent until now, finally entered into the conversation as a peacemaker. "You aren't going to settle this today, so enough of this serious talk. Why don't you ladies fix some sandwiches and something cold to drink. Paul and I will meet you at the picnic table in the backyard. We need to relax—not argue."

Marie, who hated confrontations, quickly agreed, "Doug, that sounds like a great idea."

As Marie and I went into the kitchen, I thought, *Learning to trust isn't going to be easy for Paul.* At the time I had no idea how true my thoughts were, but later, after reading several more books about addiction, I learned just how difficult it is for an addict to trust. An addict feels a strong need to be in control and fears that if he trusts other people and allows them to get close to him, they will have power over him. Likely, when he was a child, his parents or other authority figures used their power in an abusive way, shattering his trust. Now, as an adult, he is determined not to lose his power to other people by trusting them and will often intentionally end a relationship that gets too close.

As my knowledge and understanding of sexual addiction grew, I began to accept it as an illness, and I also came to believe that Paul was a Christian when he committed the sex offenses. Does anyone doubt that a Christian can have a cold, a broken arm, or cancer? Why, then, can't that same Christian suffer from a mental or emotional illness? Yes, molesting a child is a sin, but don't all of us sin in one way or another? Isn't all illness a direct result of Adam's original sin?

I despise the cancer that caused my mother's death, but I certainly didn't hate her because she had the cancer. I loved her but hated the cancer. We should always hate the pain that sexual addiction inflicts on both the addict and the victim, but we should also follow Jesus' example and show them compassion and understanding. As Christians we are commanded to love the sinner but hate the sin. To do this may take a superhuman effort, but we have a supernatural God who has covered all of our sins with the righteousness of Jesus.

· 10 ·

Child Molestation

Oh, please, show the great power [of your patience]
by forgiving our sins and showing us your steadfast love.
Forgive us, even though you have said that you don't let sin
go unpunished, and that you punish the father's fault in the
children to the third and fourth generation.
Numbers 14: 17–18

I spent the next few days specifically concentrating my research on the problem of child molestation. Again, I believe it was best to start with a definition of *child molestation*. I found an accurate description in a book by Anna Saltzor entitled, *Treating Child Sex Offenders and Victims.* Child molestation is:

sexual activity between a child or adolescent with an adult or another child five years or more older than the child. Sexual activity will include exhibitionism, voyeurism, fondling, oral genital sex, attempted intercourse, "dry" intercourse (rubbing the penis between the thighs or buttocks of a child), intercourse, photographing or otherwise exhibiting children sexually, exposing children to pornographic literature, and forcing or manipulating children to engage in sexual acts with each other or with animals. Sexual experiences with relatives and violent or coerced experiences will be automatically considered sexual abuse regardless of the age differential. There are exceptions to the age-differential criterion when common sense will indicate that a particular situation is abusive, for example, manipulated consent of a retarded child by a non-retarded child of a similar age.[1]

Just reading the definition disturbed me. It's no wonder society has so little sympathy for the offender. And yet, what does the general public really know about the subject?

The inaccurate image most people have in their minds of a child molester actually enables that person to be more effective in committing his sexual offenses. Many see the molester as being different from other people. Their misconception is that the offender is a sex fiend, a dirty old man, or a sexually frustrated woman—someone with low self-esteem and a strange personality who is sexually unattractive to others. They may picture the offender as someone who lurks around playgrounds and dark alleys with a sinister look on his face. In reality, the child molester could be you, me, or a neighbor. The offender may be illiterate or highly educated, poor or rich, able or disabled, gay or straight, employed or unemployed, a blue-collar or white-collar worker, responsible or irresponsible, a person of color or a Caucasian, a criminal with an extensive record or someone who has never even received a parking ticket, religious or nonreligious, extrovert or introvert, attractive or homely. Frequently a child molester is a respected person—someone with charisma, charm, and extraordinary social and sexual skills, liked by both children and adults.

The community was shocked when Paul was arrested because he didn't fit their image of a sex offender. "Many people assume if you have a particular sexual orientation, such as the desire for children sexually, that you are 'bad' in terms of your traits of character—that you do not care about others, that you are irresponsible in your vocation, that you have perhaps a long history of truancy and delinquency, and so forth. That is not at all necessarily true. You may be a very responsible person but happen to be afflicted."[2]

Whenever a child is molested, an outraged public cries out, "Why?" Obviously, if there were an answer to their question, the problem could be controlled or eliminated. Parents, older siblings, relatives, physicians, day care workers, scout leaders, playground coordinators, teachers, friends, clergy, babysitters, camp counselors, lifeguards, and many others exploit children sexually. Most professionals who deal with sexual abuse, sexual offending, and sexual addiction conservatively estimate that one out of every three girls and one in every four boys is sexually molested before their eighteenth birthday. The majority of children are molested in their own homes and backyards by those in a position of trust. Parents should also be alert to danger wherever children, teenagers, and young adults work, play, or congregate. A child molester will often gravitate to an occupation that brings him in direct contact with children.

Some experts believe that characterological immaturity can be a contributing factor. "The addict who focuses on children usually has suffered some interruption in his or her own development while growing up. There is a part of the addict which is not any older than the victim."[3]

Paul is attracted to girls between twelve and sixteen years of age. That is within the same age range as the two girls who molested him as a child, giving him, for the first time in his life, a feeling of acceptance and belonging. He learned from his experience with the girls that it was okay for an older person to have sex with a child. Today, in his recovery, he is learning to find acceptance and belonging in relationships that are not based solely on sex.

Some experts believe that sexual compulsivity may be hereditary—passed on from one generation to the next. However, others feel that it is a learned process, passed on by teaching, not genes. "It is known that many people who as children were sexually abused by adults do the same thing when they grow up. Also children who were severely punished physically or who grew up in an emotionally unhappy home may be more likely to become child molesters."[4]

Both heredity and learned behavior appear to have played a part in Paul's case. Paul told me that in his family there were other relatives whose behavior indicated sexual addiction might be present. He recalled how, when he was a young teenager, his stepmother made him accompany her and his dad to the home of a young woman. When they arrived, he waited in the car while they went inside. On the drive home, he found out from their heated conversation that his dad had been sexually involved with one of the girls who lived there and had also tried to talk her younger sister into having sex with him. She objected and told her older sister who, in turn, called Paul's stepmother.

Anything that lowers a person's inhibitions and self-control, such as alcohol, drugs, or stress, can cause a sex addict to act out. For months prior to his arrest, Paul was severely depressed because his employer had been treating him unfairly. He was also approaching his fiftieth birthday which, due to his sensitivity to aging, added to his depression. Frequently a sex offender inappropriately converts normal nonsexual problems, such as work difficulties and aging, into a pattern of improper sexual behavior.

In a book entitled *Retraining Adult Sex Offenders: Methods and Models*, Richard Laws, a behaviorist and social-learning theorist and founder of the Sexual Behavior Laboratory at

Atascardero State Hospital in California, is quoted as saying that some early life events become learned behavior and begin to shape the sexually aggressive patterns of paraphiliacs. A paraphiliac is a person who has characteristic compulsive thoughts and urges to carry out sexually aggressive behaviors. This is usually the only area of his life that is out of control. Mr. Laws goes on to say, "I am a strong believer in social learning, and these folks learn how to become pedophiles, they learn how to become rapists. . . . You can't really find sexual activities with a 12-year-old girl attractive just by thinking about it. You don't have preparation, you haven't been socialized to believe that that behavior is either an acceptable or a desirable thing. You have to really engage in the behavior and learn how to do it. . . . These persons spend hours and hours planning sex offenses."[5]

All of the contributing factors I have mentioned simply suggest why a sex offender, such as Paul, might have made incorrect choices in dealing with his sexuality. There is never an acceptable excuse for a person to molest a child or engage in any compulsive behavior that injures himself or others. The sex offender must decide whether his own feelings of desire, rejection, frustration, loneliness, anger, and low self-worth are more important than the feelings of his victim. The offender must come to realize that he might obtain a false rush or high caused by the pleasure of the moment, but the consequences of his actions will harm the victim for a lifetime. All perpetrators must learn to take responsibility for their actions and learn to live with the consequences caused by them.

· 11 ·

The Arraignment

And remember that your heavenly Father to whom you
pray has no favorites when he judges.
1 Peter 1:17

Doug and I continued to pray for Paul and Marie's marriage. Although Marie had considered going to an attorney to obtain a divorce, she hadn't done so yet. She hated the finality of taking the legal steps needed to initiate the divorce process. Most of the time she and Paul communicated through verbal battles, but Doug and I noticed that their fights were about anything and everything except the real issue—Paul's sexual addiction and offenses. Marie's drawn, tense face and shattered nerves concerned us, but with God's help and taking one day at a time, she persevered. I could sense her fear of the unknown, her apprehension about what lay ahead. But for now, she appeared to be content to just place her life on hold until after the arraignment and sentencing. On more than one occasion I said to her, "Marie, slow down—there's no need to rush. The decisions that you make now are going to affect you and your family for the rest of your lives."

One afternoon, a week before Paul's arraignment, I called him to come in to lunch. He reluctantly stopped his painting and joined me in the kitchen. I was astonished at how, outwardly at least, he didn't appear to be worried about the arraignment. "I don't understand how you can be so calm," I said. "Are you that confident?"

"The uncertainty has been hanging over my head for almost four months. I just want it to end! Besides," he said with resignation, "I'm powerless. The judge's decision is out of my hands. Either he will accept my plea bargain or he won't." He then quoted a part of the Serenity Prayer to me— a prayer used by those following a twelve-step program to gain strength during times of need: "Lord, grant me the serenity to accept the things I cannot change, the courage to change the things I can, and the wisdom to know the difference."

I smiled as I placed a bowl of chili before him. "Paul, you've come a long way!"

"True, but I still have a long way to go before I'll be well. In my twelve-step group, we have a saying: 'Sober isn't well. *Sober* means that there is to be no sex of any kind with yourself or a partner, other than your heterosexual spouse. I've been sexually sober since my arrest, so I've started my recovery, but I'm far from well. I constantly remind myself that I'm going to be a sex addict for the rest of my life."

"Paul, you may be a sex addict, but Doug and I are convinced that you don't belong in jail."

This time he smiled—something he rarely did. "You know, Beth, I sure wish one of the Sterlings could be my judge!"

By this time Paul had completed 99 percent of the outside work, including painting the house. All that was left to do were a few small projects he had deliberately not finished. Doug and I began to wonder if we would have to complete them. Paul hadn't totally finished the outside of the house before he was busy painting the inside.

The days before his arraignment, Paul was working in our dining room. I had gone upstairs to get some papers from the den and observed that he had finished painting the ceiling. He had cleaned and replaced the blades on the ceiling fan and was now putting the globes back on the light fixture. "The ceiling looks great," I said, forgetting that he didn't like to be complimented. Then I added, "Be careful you don't get hit by the fan; maybe you should turn it off until you've finished working around it."

Just as I was entering the den, I heard a loud, cracking noise. At first I thought the sound had come from outside, but then I remembered—Paul was working on the fan. *Don't be silly*, I thought. *If the fan had hit him, he would be yelling. Besides, the noise I just heard was too loud to have been caused by a fan hitting something.* Then I heard him calmly call me. "Beth, would you please come out here—I need you."

Was I ever wrong! When I got to the dining room, I found a pale and dazed Paul, sitting in a chair, holding his head. Blood from a large cut above his left eye was oozing out from between his fingers, running down his face onto his clothes.

"Your fan attacked me," he said with a feeble attempt at humor.

Somehow I managed to help him to the bathroom where he washed the blood from his face and I poured hydrogen peroxide into the wound. Then, in an attempt to stop the bleeding, I put a towel and ice pack on it.

"Paul, this cut is deep! You're going to need stitches. We've got to get you to a doctor." I was also concerned that he might have a concussion from the force of the blow. Remembering the horrible sound I'd heard earlier, I shuddered.

He didn't argue with me about going to a doctor.

Thank God, he didn't have a concussion, but eighteen stitches were required to close the cut. In addition to the big bump, or "goose egg" as he called it, he also had a very ugly looking black eye.

"This mess on my face is all I need to impress the judge tomorrow! I look like I've been in a bar fight," he said sarcastically.

I had to agree. "Can't your attorney tell him what happened?"

"Of course she can. I can just hear her saying, 'Your Honor, won't you please excuse my client's appearance. He ran into a ceiling fan. It's obvious who won.'"

That evening, while Paul was attending his twelve-step meeting, Doug and I discussed his case.

"You have to admit," I said, "that black eye isn't going to help his confidence. But you don't think it will influence the judge, do you?"

"If the judge wants to know how he got it, I'm sure he'll ask."

"What do you think will happen tomorrow?"

"That the plea bargain will be accepted—but it could be that I believe it just because I want to."

"Touching the girls was inexcusable, but at least Paul didn't have sex with them. And it's also his first offense. Surely the judge will take all that into consideration."

"Even more importantly," Doug added, "he's receiving help—he recognizes his problem."

"Paul told me about a friend of his who recently began a prison sentence of five to ten years for molesting his fifteen-year-old stepdaughter. The girl apparently initiated the sexual contact with her stepfather, and Paul was upset because he thought that her actions should have influenced the decision of the court."

"It can't, because no matter what the child does, the adult always has the responsibility for setting proper boundaries. He should have said no to her, no matter what the circumstances."

"That's true," I agreed, walking to my desk and picking up a reference book. "This paragraph plainly spells it out," I said, quoting from *Treating Child Sex Offenders and Victims* by Anna Saltzer.

> A child who engages in sexual activity with an adult through ignorance, confusion, manipulation, fear, or psychological dependency should not be labeled "participating," with the implication that the child sought and willingly continued the sexual relationship. The fact that an offender gained repeated access to the child is evidence not of the child's planning and persistence in the deviant behavior but of the offender's. If that child then generalizes the behavior and approaches other adults as she has been taught, to exchange sex for affection, it would seem unsupportable to label her as "provocative," rather than as injured by her experiences.[1]

"From what I've heard and read," Doug said thoughtfully, "a child who has never been molested doesn't usually initiate sex with an adult. But, if they are starving for love, I suppose they might." He continued, "It's really not important how it starts or if the child willingly participates. What is important is that any child who has been molested should receive counseling."

"I agree. It should be required by law. If Paul had gotten help years ago, maybe he wouldn't be going to court tomorrow. Maybe he would have learned how to appropriately express his affection for children."

"The way some young girls dress and act, it's sometimes difficult to tell a child from an adult. Beth, I've never told you about this before, but when I was in the navy, an officer on my ship invited me to his home for dinner. Shortly after I arrived, he asked me to take his twelve-year-old daughter to the playground while he helped his wife prepare dinner. When we got to the playground, it was deserted; we were the only ones there. Without warning, the girl started coming on to me—strong. She asked me to do it to her and assured me that I wouldn't be the first. She also promised she wouldn't tell. I knew that what she wanted me to do would be wrong; she was underage, and I could go to jail. The thought of jail made saying no easier, but I have to admit, she was attractive, fully developed, and very mature. She looked and acted like a woman—but, in reality, she was just a mixed-up kid."

I sighed. "Doug, apparently there are a lot of mixed-up kids in the world. In yesterday's paper I read an article that said one out of every five American children lose their virginity before they are thirteen. These children come from all kinds of homes—both Christian and non-Christian."

Doug sadly shook his head. "Kids reach puberty, and their hormones refuse to be put on hold."

"True," I said, glancing at my watch. "Before it gets any later, I think I'll call Marie to see how she's doing. I imagine she and Paul are nervous about tomorrow."

She answered on the third ring. "Are you worried?" I asked.

"I don't know what I feel—or if I feel." She sighed. "It's just one more hurdle to get past. After that comes the sentencing."

"But if they accept his plea bargain, the sentencing will just be a formality. Right?"

"Not really. The judge doesn't have to accept the plea bargain and can change his mind at the last minute."

Oh great! I thought. *Our legal system can dangle you indefinitely.*

"Well, I just wanted to let you know that Doug and I have been praying for you both. Please call us and let us know as soon as you hear what happens."

"Beth, I won't be going to the arraignment. Paul doesn't want me to and . . . well . . . I don't believe I can handle much more." She seemed apologetic.

"That's probably best for you—I'm sure Paul is concerned about you and doesn't want you to be embarrassed."

Her tone became defensive. "It's his embarrassment—not mine! I'm not the one who did something wrong. Besides, Shirley insists that she's going to go with him, and you know her, once she makes up her mind, there's no point in arguing."

I smiled. "That's true. She has a way of intimidating people." *But,* I thought, *wherever Shirley is, there also is her contagious faith. She'll be good for Paul.*

The next morning I had difficulty concentrating on my work. *You've become too involved,* I thought. I also was emotionally torn. I didn't want Paul to go to jail, but at the same time, I wanted the victims to see our justice system work for them—to realize that their cries had been heard. They had been courageous to report Paul.

Most victims remain silent—for various reasons. Often, it's because they've been warned not to tell. Most children have been taught to obey and respect an adult, and even though they know that what is being done to them is wrong, they don't know what to do about it. A molester will try to convince the children that if they do tell, no one will believe them—that they will be blamed. They use threats, bribes, and sometimes even the word *love* to accomplish their objective. Many times, in cases of parental incest, the children have been convinced by the offending parent that if they tell, they will be responsible for sending them to jail. Then, with mommy or daddy gone, who would be there to care and provide for them? Also, most children feel guilt and shame if they think that they cooperated with or enjoyed the sexual abuse. When children are asked and don't say no, they feel they have cooperated. If they respond to a pleasant feeling, they may feel they have done something wrong because they enjoyed it. Such feelings may interfere with their ability to express anger toward their abuser. But again it must be emphasized that, no matter what, it is *never* permissible for an adult to have any kind of sexual contact with a child.

Children who have suffered sexual abuse over a long period of time feel different from their friends and believe that they are alone in their situation. Victims may be frightened but, at the same time, admit only to themselves that some of the feelings were nice. Insecure children may literally offer their body to a stranger in order to receive the affection that is craved. They don't realize that they are entitled to receive love without abuse. Whenever money or gifts are given to the children, they may feel special, but it can also start them on the road to sexual manipulation and sometimes prostitution. In contrast, other children may feel guilt and shame because they didn't know how to stop the molester. They blame the offender for making them feel different.

When I first told my parents about Mr. Stephens, they ignored the situation. At the other extreme are the parents who show such excessive emotional reaction that they may actually add to the child's problem. Their extreme reaction often causes more psychological and emotional harm to the child than the actual abuse. Suppose, for example, the victim overhears her parents talking about the long-lasting effects of her ordeal. She may hear her parents threaten to kill the offender for the pain and shame caused to the family. For weeks or even months the child may be repeatedly asked if she is experiencing any nightmares about the abuse. The child could begin to feel guilty because she isn't experiencing the adverse reaction the parents are expecting. Soon she begins to wonder, *How come I'm not feeling the way I'm supposed to?*

Parents cannot and should not ignore what happened to their child, nor should they allow their emotions to get out of control. Experts believe parents should encourage their child to talk freely, expressing any fears and concerns she may have. They should show comfort, sympathy, support, and love, using confidence-building words to reinforce within the child a positive self-image. Parents should remember that their outlook influences their child's outlook! Insist that the child initially be evaluated by a trained professional who can determine if long-term counseling is needed. A child who has been sexually abused over a long period of time may attempt to hide the pain of the abuse by assuming a separate personality. This is the only way she knows how to protect the other child—the one that is being abused. There is no other way she can run away.

Why hasn't Marie called? I asked myself. It was now mid-afternoon, and Paul's arraignment had been scheduled for that morning. *Was something wrong?* I wanted to call her but didn't want to tie up the phone. If someone had told me a few months earlier that I would be showing this much concern for a sex offender, I would never have believed it. I thanked God for letting me see beyond the surface.

As I was studying the characteristics of a sex addict, I came to realize that it was an accurate description of Paul. Addicts are people who have low self-esteem—manipulators who will lie to get what they want. They are suspicious, critical, untrusting, domineering, fearful, and angry. The majority of addicts come from alcoholic or other dysfunctional homes where the parents were either separated or divorced. Many addicts were sexually, physically, and/or emotionally abused or neglected and didn't do well in school. As adults, they are bored and do not know how to have a deep, meaningful relationship; they see intimacy as being strictly sexual. Most likely, they had established a pattern of sexually deviant behavior by their teenage years. Addicts seldom have fun; they don't know how. Fearing disapproval and rejection, a sex addict doesn't follow through on things. Love is frightening to the addict, making him feel powerless. He quickly builds emotional walls—once built, they are not easily torn down. Addicts are convinced that if people really knew them, they would be rejected. Sex addicts who have suffered sexual abuse will frequently withdraw into isolation within themselves. They disassociate themselves by trying to hide behind their self-built walls in a futile attempt to keep others out.

When Marie called, she sounded relieved. "It's over. The judge has agreed to his plea bargain."

"Thank God!"

"He'll be on probation for two years, and he'll have to continue going to his twelve-step meetings and see Bill twice a week for counseling. And he'll be leaving for Texas in four days."

"Texas?"

"Yes, for thirty days. He'll be a patient in the RAPHA unit of the Hill Country Psychiatric Hospital in San Antonio."

"I think Paul mentioned it to me. Isn't it a Christian facility?"

"Yes," she said. "Their brochure says that they provide Christ-centered, inpatient treatment for those suffering from psychiatric and addictive problems." She paused. "Bill told him that it's the best place to go for help. All the therapists are Christians."

"That's great, Marie; I'm sure that going there will be a big step in his recovery!"

"Recovery," she repeated. "I'm not sure if either one of us will ever fully recover."

Later, when Paul returned, he expressed his gratitude and a sense of hope. "Pray that the doctors at the hospital will be able to help me. It doesn't matter what they do, or how they do it—just so they help me get my life under control."

"They will," I said, feeling optimistic.

A frown crossed his face. "I'm sure there will be another write-up in the paper tomorrow. Once again Marie will have to endure people staring at her accusingly and be the object of their pity and scorn. And then there's Ann—she'll probably be teased and picked on by the other kids at school."

"Were there any reporters there?"

"A few—also, a lot of spectators. But there were some delays in the cases ahead of mine, so by the time my case came up, the courtroom was practically empty. That . . . that made it easier for me. I was spared seeing all those disapproving faces glaring at me, crucifying me with their hatred."

"At least this time Marie won't receive any nasty phone calls," I said. "You were smart to get an unlisted number."

"But she still has to go to work every day—and some of her coworkers are so hateful and mean to her! Beth, will you pray with me that the publicity won't be too bad? Marie is near the breaking point, and it isn't going to take much more for our shaky marriage to be totally shattered. Only God knows how important it is to me to keep my marriage and family together."

And so the two of us prayed, and then later on when Doug came home, the three of us prayed again.

As always, God was faithful. The next day we scanned the pages of Paul's local newspaper but at first didn't find anything about his arraignment. We looked again—this time more carefully—and finally spotted a short paragraph buried in the middle pages, sandwiched insignificantly between other reports. We were jubilant.

"Now you need to concentrate on getting ready for your trip to Texas."

"Emotionally, I'm ready—I have been for a long time!"

The day after his arraignment, Paul and I went grocery shopping. When we arrived, the store was crowded, but it didn't bother me because I had stopped worrying about who might see me with Paul. I had come to accept him for what he was now—not what he had been. Ever since his arraignment, he had been in good spirits and couldn't wait to get on the plane to Texas. *It's good to see him looking forward to something*, I thought.

We were methodically going up and down the aisles, joking as we began to fill our cart. "You're out of teabags," Paul said.

"And detergent."

"How's the sugar supply?"

"I think it's getting low."

I had taken the cart and gone ahead to the pet section to pick up dog food for Dusty, our Lhasa apso. Paul was following a short distance behind, systematically checking out the shelves.

As I was placing the dog food in the cart, his voice interrupted me. "Beth, look who I found following us up and down the aisles. It's Susan—Sue Chambers."

When I turned around, I was surprised to see Sue, an attractive, young woman whom I knew from my former church. Apparently, she had stopped going to the church a short time after Doug and I left. Although, in all likelihood, she was aware of Paul's arrest, it was obvious from the flushed, embarrassed look on her face that she had no idea he had been staying with us.

"She has her new baby with her," Paul said, pointing to the little one. She had been pregnant when we left the church.

I must have told her at least ten times how cute her baby girl was. It was the only thing I could think of to say.

Paul asked Susan about the rest of her family and also commented on how cute her baby was.

We were all uncomfortable—but, at the same time, I was struck by the humor of it.

I began to wonder what she was thinking. Paul and I were together—he, the former deacon, recently arrested for sexual offenses, and I, the Christian publisher and Bible student, the wife of another former deacon. And it was obvious that he and I were enjoying ourselves, laughing as we filled the grocery cart.

As we were talking, I saw her look suspiciously at Paul's black eye and stitches. Her imagination must have been running rampant—it seemed so probable—Paul had obviously moved in with me. Apparently, after Doug found out about us, he had punched him in the eye. Now, here we were, out shopping together.

"Your baby sure is cute," Paul said again.

"She sure is," I agreed, trying to come up with a way to end the conversation gracefully.

Why doesn't he explain why we are together? I wondered.

"I'll be going to Texas," Paul said. "I'm going to be there for thirty days of treatment."

Good opening, I thought. That is until I saw Susan's reaction to the word *treatment.* She looked very uncomfortable, so after telling her how nice it was to see her again, we hurried to put some distance between us. Once we were sure she was far enough away, we discussed what had just happened. We agreed that it was funny but, if left uncorrected, could have serious consequences.

"We can't let this go without explaining it to her," I said. "When we get home, I'll give her a call. Her face sure got a strange look on it when she saw we were together."

"I'm sure that look wasn't because we were together—but because of me. Ever since my arrest, people are nervous around me and don't know what to say."

"It didn't help when she saw us both putting groceries in the same cart."

"Beth, I think you're right. You'd better call her. I don't want to be responsible for ruining your reputation."

"Look at it this way," I teased, "it probably helped yours."

"I'm not so sure about that!" Paul jokingly replied.

I considered our conversation to be healthy. When I had first learned that Paul had been involved with adult women, I became uneasy. Until that time, Tina had been my only concern. Also, the threat of a possible jail sentence hanging over his head gave me a further sense of reassurance. He would be stupid if he tried anything . . . and he wasn't stupid! Nevertheless, I had watched him carefully. But it became clear that he had respect for our friendship and understood its boundaries. Some sex addicts find it difficult, if not impossible, to have a nonsexual friendship with a woman, but Paul told me about several women with whom he had enjoyed a genuine friendship. Yet he found it almost impossible to form such a friendship with a man, probably because he never felt close to his father and didn't know how to relate.

Paul had finished painting the inside of our home except for one bedroom. He said he would try to finish it before leaving for Texas, but I assured him that if he didn't, Doug and I would. However, I did ask him to please complete all the other projects he had started and not finished. "You haven't finished painting one small section of the front of our house," I said. "The limbs you trimmed off the apple trees need to be cut and stacked, and you haven't finished grouting the tile around the shower in the bathroom. It will only take you a few hours to complete these things—a day at most."

When he didn't reply, I continued, "Paul, you've done a great job with everything. . . . There, I've said it to you; the worst is now over—you've been complimented and survived. So, after you've completed all these loose ends, I won't say another word."

"Beth, you've been reading too many psychology books—you've started reading my mind."

"I don't have to; your face tells it all."

"There's something I want to ask you," he said.

"Okay."

"Are you still afraid to leave your daughter alone with me?"

I knew he didn't really want to be alone with Tina—that he was testing me to see how much I trusted him. "Paul, I know you're better now than when you first came to stay with us, but you're still an addict with an addiction that's difficult to control. Perhaps, someday, after you've been in recovery longer, I'll . . . I'll feel differently."

He didn't reply, but I saw him smile slightly.

Two days later, Paul prepared to leave for the airport. Doug was to drive him there before continuing on to his office. Paul hugged me as he was leaving, and I promised that I would write to him. How I prayed that when he came back from Texas, he could return to his own home—to his wife and little girl. Now that his arraignment was over, he could move back home if Marie agreed, but she still had to work things out within herself. For weeks Doug and I had been praying that their marriage would survive. We were acutely aware that many women divorce a husband who has been found guilty of molesting a child. But Marie was spiritually strong—and from what she had told me in our conversations, she loved him. However, it remained to be seen whether that love would be strong enough to overcome her feelings of betrayal and anger.

Aware that Marie might not allow him to return to their home after his hospitalization in Texas, Paul called his hometown area and made temporary arrangements to stay with friends who lived near the counseling center. His next step would be to look for an apartment.

✦ 12 ✦

Excuses and Symptoms

*A man without self-control is as defenseless
as a city with broken-down walls.*
Proverbs 25:28

Even though Paul was no longer in our home, my research continued. The publishing business kept me extremely busy, but all my spare moments were used to investigate the complex problems of sexual addiction and sex offenders.

I found that addicts and sex offenders rationalize their behavior in an attempt to justify their actions. For example, some common excuses a child molester might use are:

I'm simply providing sex education for her. After all, she has to learn sometime.

It's better for her to learn about sex from an expert like me than from someone her own age who doesn't know what they're doing.

Since she didn't say no, she must want to do it.

She willingly sat on my lap and put her arms around me, so she must really want this love and affection.

It's okay because she looks and acts older than she really is.

She told me she's done it before, so it doesn't matter if I do it too.

She's so young that she won't know what I'm doing and probably won't remember it.

She'll enjoy it more now because she knows she's too young to get pregnant.

I learned about sex when I was her age, so why shouldn't she? I survived, so I know it won't kill her.

It's okay because she's my daughter, and as a parent, I have a duty to teach her.

She told me no, but I know that she really meant yes.

I'll only do it this one time—it won't hurt her—she'll soon forget all about it.

I'm smart and if I'm careful I won't get caught. No one will ever know about it.

I'll take her to nice places she normally wouldn't get the chance to see.

I'll buy her special presents—things she likes but can't afford.

She enjoys being with me because she knows how much I love children.

She must like me doing it to her or she wouldn't ask me to tuck her in every night.

It's only my stepdaughter or adopted daughter—she's not my real daughter—so it's not really incest.

I'll just look at her—nothing else.

All girls enjoy doing it, and I know that after a while she will too.

I'll only touch her and not use force—what harm will it do?

God must agree with what I'm doing because, when I asked, he didn't take my desire away.

I've tried, but I'm a weak person and just can't help myself!

She's smiling—it shows she likes it.

It's okay because, in all areas of my life except this one, I'm a very good person.

She tempted me and led me on.

She told me she'd done it before or expressed curiosity about it and asked me to show her how to do it.

I'll teach her so she'll know exactly what she should not allow someone else to do to her.

What I do in my home is my business and no one else's.

It's difficult to recognize an adult who was sexually abused as a child. However, a sexually abused child can more easily be identified—even by a nonprofessional. "Sexually abused children show a variety of sexual symptoms that range from a preoccupation with sex to fear and avoidance of any aspect of sexuality."[1]

When a nonabused child plays "doctor," he or she will pretend to take a temperature, set a broken bone, or prescribe fake pills. In contrast, a child who has been sexually abused will look intimately at his or her own or another child's body, touching and feeling private places, often inserting a finger or an object into the vagina or anal opening. If sexual intercourse or attempted intercourse was part of the sexual abuse suffered by the child, it's not unusual for him or her to then do the same with other children.

Abused children may be depressed, nervous, or shy, and may be extremely vulnerable to a sexual approach from an adult or another child. They often have a poor self-image, self-esteem, and self-worth. They have difficulty trusting and, at first, may appear to be slow learners or mentally handicapped. Often they run away from home or try to escape through the use of alcohol, drugs, or even more sex.

We must face the reality that there are child molesters living within our communities. It's important that we try to learn as much as we can about these offenders so that the risk of our children becoming victims is minimized. However, the general public should not be required to change the way they live because of the danger posed by this criminal element in our society.

I have a life-threatening allergy to walnuts, pecans, and other nuts. My allergic reaction is so severe that I literally could die within minutes after eating a nut—or even from touching a nutshell. Needless to say, I avoid these morsels of death as if they were the plague, carefully checking out the ingredients in all packaged and prepared foods. In a restaurant, if there is a possible problem with a particular item on the menu, I ask to speak with the chef. For me, it would be wonderful if all nuts in the world were banned from human consumption. That would mean everyone else would have to be willing to give up eating nuts in order to protect me—but, of course, that would be unrealistic.

It is also totally unrealistic to expect our society to change its way of living just to protect itself from the threat of sex offenders. For example, church directories, school activity lists, and names printed in the newspaper are but a few of the sources that can provide a molester with the name, address, age, telephone number, interests, and other specific information about young people. Should we deny our newspapers the right to honor our children by placing their names and pictures in the paper? Should we refuse to have their names and phone numbers printed in our church directories? Should we forbid our children to place an ad in a store or the newspaper to obtain a job as a baby-sitter? It's my opinion that we should not stop doing these things. All parents should be aware, however, that there are many legitimate sources a molester may use to obtain a child's name and address. Individual parents may decide to withhold their children's names from all directories and newspapers, but it's not feasible to expect all parents to do the same. If we were to do so, we would allow our actions to be controlled and manipulated by the child molester because he is unable to control his own actions.

A sex addict who becomes sexually involved with an adult or compulsively acts out sexually in other ways will also rationalize and make excuses for his behavior. Some common excuses are:

I can't help it—I'm oversexed.
She's asking for it and wants it as bad as I do.
It's my way of relaxing.
All guys take what they can.
Men need it more often than women.
My wife is frigid.
My wife doesn't understand me.
She acts like she doesn't want to, but I know she really does.
With all the stress I've been under, I deserve this.
As long as my wife doesn't know about it, it won't hurt her.
Love isn't involved, so what I'm doing isn't infidelity.
If she didn't want me to look, she wouldn't leave her shades up.
It's not really my fault; I just had too much to drink.
I'm in love again!
I'll just go so far and then stop.
She was hitchhiking and should have known what to expect.
I didn't plan it—it just happened.
If I have an affair, my wife will no longer have to do her duty.
Something that feels this good can't be wrong.

Sex with her is more exciting than with my wife.

Having sex makes me feel good about myself.

My wife doesn't love me, so I'm entitled to take love wherever and whenever I can find it.

My wife cheated on me, so I'm just getting even with her.

Everyone knows that there are more women than men in the world—I'm just helping out all those poor women who don't have a man.

She enjoyed looking when I exposed myself.

It isn't pornography—it's art.

The more sexual experience I get, the better lover I'll be for my wife.

God must have wanted it to happen because he brought us together.

Statistics show that everyone else is doing it, so why shouldn't I?

My wife let herself go—she isn't attractive anymore.

I don't want to hurt her feelings or break her heart by turning her down—no woman likes to be told no.

The poor girl needed the money, and I was lonely and needed her—so we made a fair trade.

It doesn't count because, even though we did everything else, we didn't have complete intercourse.

It she didn't want a sex partner, why was she walking the streets alone at night?

My wife is physically and/or emotionally ill, and either doesn't want to or can't meet my needs.

It's important that a sex addict or offender recognize the consequences of his actions and take full responsibility for them. He must see these types of excuses exactly for what they are—an attempt to explain away his behavior. Recognizing the denial and rationalization processes that he uses is vital to his recovery.

✦ 13 ✦

Diagnosis

For the time is coming when the truth will be revealed:
their secret plots will become public information.

Matthew 10:26

During the month Paul was in Texas, Marie and I became better acquainted. My concern for her increased as I became aware of her fragile emotional state. It was difficult for her to relax—even to sit down long enough to drink a cup of coffee. Her nursing job kept her busy, but even during her nonworking hours, she was still continually on the go, grasping at any excuse to keep moving. It would take her an hour to drive to our house, but shortly after arriving, she would begin to pace the floor and then in a few more minutes be ready to leave. She reminded me of a caged hamster on a wheel. Always in a hurry to get someplace—running in circles—never stopping. *God*, I thought. *Please do something; she can't continue like this. Help her deal with it.*

From what she shared with me, it didn't sound as if she were planning to let Paul return home. *More time*, I thought, *they need more time.*

I found that we were beginning to talk more and more about Paul's many good qualities, and less and less about the bad things he had done. Whenever an opportunity presented itself, I would gently remind her that, although he was sick, he was also receiving help for his illness.

One day Marie said to me, "My marriage will never be the same."

"No," I replied, "it won't be—but if you work at it, it could be even better."

She gave me a puzzled look.

"Marie, your marriage has never been real. Paul was playing a role—leading a double life. Now, God's giving you another opportunity to begin again with everything out in the open."

"I'll never be able to trust him! He might do it again!"

"That's true—but, other than Jesus, nothing in life carries a guarantee."

"Beth, if this had happened to you—if Doug were the guilty person—would you take him back?"

"I . . . I honestly don't know. But I do know that I'd want to give our marriage every possible chance. I think I'd probably take him back. One thing for sure, I know I'd do a lot of praying."

"I've prayed continually since Paul's arrest. I read Psalm 139 often to remind me that God hears my every word—that I'm important to him."

"And that knowledge is going to help you get through this."

"Not 'going to,' it has! I don't know about the future, but God is the only reason I've stayed with Paul this far. You see,

Beth, one afternoon shortly after his arrest, I was so depressed that I decided to lay down on my bed and read my Bible. I was looking for answers, but God was silent. Tears blurred my vision, so I placed my Bible on the bed beside me. Suddenly, an emotional dam broke within me and my tears changed to sobs. It was awful! Eventually I cried myself to sleep. Something wonderful happened when I woke up! My Bible was open to Second Corinthians. I had not been reading Corinthians earlier. When I looked down at chapter 2, the words in verses 5 through 11 seemed to jump out at me. Beth, it was just incredible!"

"Well, come on," I said, "what does it say?"

"Rather than try and tell you, I'd prefer to read it. Can I borrow your Bible?"

As I retrieved my Bible from a nearby bookcase, she again repeated with emphasis that her Bible had *not* been open to Corinthians when she fell asleep.

As she read the verses, her voice was unsteady.

If anyone has caused grief, he has not so much grieved me as he has grieved all of you, to some extent—not to put it too severely. The punishment inflicted on him by the majority is sufficient for him. Now instead, you ought to forgive and comfort him, so that he will not be overwhelmed by excessive sorrow. I urge you, therefore, to reaffirm your love for him. The reason I wrote you was to see if you would stand the test and be obedient in everything. If you forgive anyone, I also forgive him. And what I have forgiven—if there was anything to forgive—I have forgiven in the sight of Christ for your sake, in order that Satan might not outwit us. For we are not unaware of his schemes.

2 Corinthians 2: 5–11 NIV

She put the Bible down, looking at me questioningly. "Well, what do you think?"

"That God knows the desire of your heart . . . and has given you some answers. Remember, he isn't limited; he can see beyond the pain."

"I wish I could," she said.

While Paul was in Texas, Barbara and Rich, my sister and her husband, arrived from Portland, Oregon, to visit with us. One morning, soon after their arrival, Marie and Shirley stopped in to visit. After they had gone, Barb told me she could tell by the way Marie looked and acted that she was under a great deal of stress. I had told her why Paul was arrested and, as expected, she didn't show any sympathy for him. Her sympathy was for Marie, and, in typical sisterly fashion, she also had concerns about my involvement in his life.

A few days later, Marie telephoned late in the evening. I could tell by her voice that she had bad news.

"What's the matter?" I asked.

"Paul's sick and wants you or Doug to call him. There's a pay phone in his unit—he'll be waiting for your call."

"Marie, what is it? What's wrong with him?"

"They've found a tumor the size of a baseball in his neck. The biopsy report isn't back yet, but his doctor seems to think that, because of the previous radiation therapy he received to his neck, the tumor will probably be malignant."

"They're wrong—they have to be!"

"Beth, Paul's had cancer before. Years ago, he had Hodgkin's disease that involved the lymph nodes in his neck and chest. His neck was swollen, and he had such difficulty breathing that his lips would turn blue. I'll never forget—it was on our first wedding anniversary when the doctors gave us the news. They told us his life expectancy would be anywhere from a few months to, at most, two years. Fortunately, after receiving radiation therapy for thirty days, the nodes shrank and the disease went into remission. His doctors told us it was a miracle, because at that time a patient suffering from advanced Hodgkin's disease was considered terminal."

"Is this a recurrence of the Hodgkin's disease?" *If he survived cancer once,* I thought, *he can do it again.*

"It might be, but we won't know for sure until they get the results of the biopsy. However, the doctors aren't very optimistic."

"Are you okay?" I asked.

Ignoring my question, she gave me the number of the pay phone on Paul's unit. "Beth, we'd better hang up so you can call him before it gets much later."

"Okay . . . but you hang in there Marie! And don't worry, it'll work out. Call you tomorrow."

Doug had gone to bed for the night and I didn't want to disturb him, so I went into the living room and related the details of Marie's phone call to my sister and her husband.

"I'll go down to my office and use the business phone," I said, knowing that they were expecting a call from their children in Oregon.

Barb nodded. "I'll pray that God gives you the right words to say."

"He'll have to—because I sure don't have any of my own."

Nervously I dialed the number, thinking, *God, you can't let this happen—not now!*

He answered the telephone, "Hello, RAPHA unit, Paul speaking."

"Hi, Paul. It's me, Beth."

"I've been waiting for you to call. Any trouble getting through?"

"No—I just finished talking with Marie. She asked that we call you."

There was an awkward silence; then he asked, "She told you, didn't she?"

"Yes, she told me. Are you okay? Tell me the truth."

"The truth is I'm damned mad. All these medical exams and tests are eating into my time for psychiatric treatment. One of the doctors has even suggested that, medically, it might be best for me to leave here and fly home. They've already made arrangements for me to be seen by a throat specialist as soon as I get home. I've been arguing with them about leaving here earlier than planned—I'm determined to stay and complete my full thirty days of treatment. This tumor is a medical problem, but my sexual addiction is a spiritual problem that is robbing me of life itself. It's more important for me to complete my scheduled time here than come home and have this tumor removed. It didn't grow this big in just a few days, and it's not going to make any difference if it's not removed in the next few days."

"Paul, don't be ridiculous! If your doctors say so, you need to have it taken care of right away."

"Beth, either I'm going to live—or I'm going to die. The few days I have left at RAPHA aren't going to change that. What I'm learning here is life-changing. If surgery is needed, it can always be done later."

Life-changing! The words sounded great as I repeated them to myself. "Paul, it sounds as if you're really making progress. I'm sure that God hasn't brought you this far just to let you die."

His voice was shaky. "I want to be prepared for whatever happens." He paused, then continued slowly, "Beth . . . I'm not too good at saying thank you, but . . . well . . . your friendship . . . the way you and Doug have treated me . . ."

"I know," I said. And I did.

"I'm going to write down some of my favorite Bible verses and give them to you when I get home. In case I should die, would you please tell Marie I want them read at my funeral?"

Please God, I thought, *give me the words to encourage him.* "Paul, I don't believe that you're going to die. So hang in there and let God help you fight the battle."

When he spoke it was as if he hadn't heard what I said. "There's more good news—they've also told me that I'm a bipolar manic-depressive." He continued sarcastically, "Isn't that wonderful? Paul's a bipolar manic-depressive sex addict with cancer."

"It sounds scary, but you don't know for sure it's cancer. And what does this bipolar thing mean? I don't understand."

He suddenly changed the subject. "Beth, please don't finish painting that bedroom I never got to. It may take me a while, but I do intend to finish it." He deliberately emphasized his next words. "I *will* get it done, regardless."

"Okay," I said. "We won't do it."

"And please continue to pray for me!"

"We will. Every day!"

"Bye. See you in about a week. Tell Doug I'm looking forward to seeing him again."

"I will. Bye."

When I returned to the living room, Barb was watching a movie on TV. I fixed coffee for the two of us and joined her.

"Thanks," she said, as I placed a cup in front of her. Then she turned off the TV. "Beth, you're concerned about *that man* you called, aren't you?"

"Yes, I am." Then I added, "His name is Paul."

"Sis, Rich and I were talking while you were on the phone. We feel you've become too involved with this couple. When you consider all the stress you've endured over the last couple of years, it doesn't seem wise for you to get involved with another person who has cancer."

I knew she was referring to my mother-in-law, who had died a horrible death from lung cancer. When we were told that Doug's mom had only a few months left to live, I drove to West Virginia and took care of her until her death. For five months, except on weekends when they came to visit, I was separated from my family. It was a difficult time for all of us.

"Don't worry, I won't volunteer to serve as a nurse again. Besides, Paul's wife is a nurse; she can take care of him."

"But will she? From what she said, I don't think their marriage is very secure."

"But if he's sick, she won't turn her back on him. I know her; she wouldn't do that. My bet is that when he returns, he'll move back home."

"Why would she be willing to take him back? Out of a sense of duty? Or because of love?"

"Either . . . or both. I realize his illness is going to complicate things for Marie—especially because she works—but I'm convinced he belongs with his family. They've been married for over twenty-eight years and have made many memories together. Love isn't something you can easily turn on or off."

"Nor are his problems!"

"I know. He . . . he told me he's been diagnosed as a bipolar manic-depressive. You're a nurse, Barb, what does that mean?"

"Bipolar is becoming a popular term for labeling this illness. It means that Paul is suffering from a chemical imbalance in his brain that causes his emotions to swing from one extreme to the other. When he acts as though he's on top of the world, speaks rapidly, and has a high level of energy, he is in a manic stage. But when he rapidly plunges into a depression so severe that he doesn't want to talk or even get out of bed, he is in a depressed stage."

"How long do these up and down cycles last?" I asked.

"The severity and length varies with each individual. Some people have rapid mood swings many times in a day, while others may be in a high or manic cycle for months or years and then go through a low or depressed state for months or years. Some people are manic only and never go into the depressed state, while other people are always in a depressed state and never become manic. The word *bipolar* means that they cycle from manic to depressed."

"That explains some of the things I noticed when he stayed with us—his rapid speech, his excitability. He was manic."

The information provided by my sister intrigued me and spurred me to read more about this illness. I discovered that manic-depression is an illness, genetic and biochemical in nature, having to do with the way the brain processes a substance called lithium. With interest, I read that experts have found that one of the symptoms of manic-depression is hypersexuality—an increase in a person's sexual appetite that is way above normal. *Paul certainly has a great deal against him,* I thought as I read, "Such illness may in some cases be a contributory factor to the sexual offense, may compound an existing sexual abuse problem, or create a higher risk for the individual who behaves this way."[1]

Fortunately, lithium carbonate and other medications can usually bring dramatic relief for those suffering from manic-depression.

RAPHA arranged for Marie to fly to Texas for three days of counseling with Paul. When this counseling was completed, his thirty days of care came to an end, and he was discharged. He and Marie flew home together—it was now time to face the problem of the neck tumor. Even though this wasn't the ideal situation, at least they were together.

When I saw Paul, his appearance shocked me. He looked tired and much weaker than when he left. The tumor, a large lump located on the lower, front part of his neck just to the right of his Adam's apple was, according to the X-ray findings, approximately two inches thick and over five inches long. At times he would be short of breath, and at other times his voice would become hoarse and deeper than usual.

As it turned out, Paul's examination had to be rescheduled for the following weekend because the throat specialist had gone out of town.

When he called and said he was coming over to work on the unpainted room, I protested. "No way! No work for you unless your doctor says it's okay. You need to rest up for your surgery."

"Before leaving for Texas, I told you I'd paint that room—and I will."

I asked to speak with Marie. Perhaps she could talk some sense into him—get him to change his mind.

"I think he should do it," she said. "Painting won't hurt him as much as just sitting here worrying about everything. If he stays busy, maybe he won't be thinking so much about jail and cancer."

That decided it. Paul moved back in with us for a few days. He worked slowly, stopping frequently to rest and catch his breath. He acted as though he had an obsession about finishing that last room, almost as if he were in a battle with someone, fighting for control.

He talked about how he was treated in the hospital. "All the staff at RAPHA are wonderful," he said. "They really care about people. The patients participated in group and individual therapy, and as a result, we all became very close to one another."

"If you were to tell someone what helped you the most at RAPHA, what would you say?"

"Probably the greatest single thing I learned is that I am greatly loved by God and fully acceptable to him, no matter what I've done. Beth, I'm sure you're familiar with the expression, 'love the sinner but hate the sin.' Well somehow, although the meaning may be obvious to most people, I couldn't see it. But I do now, thanks to my counselors at the hospital."

"What do you mean?"

"Well, instead of saying 'love the sinner but hate the sin,' they taught me to 'love the person but hate the performance'—sinner versus sin and person versus performance. My counselor told me I'm a shame-based person—a walking ball of shame. He told me that I have been carrying so much shame in me that I will sometimes do shameful things just to prove that I am a shameful person. He then explained to me the difference between guilt and shame. Guilt is when I tell myself, 'I have done something bad and am guilty.' Shame is when I say, 'I am bad.' Guilt is how I feel about my performance—what I have done. Shame is how I feel about myself as a person—who I am.

"I learned that because I have been created in God's image I am a good person, an awesome spirit being. He loves me just as I am, in spite of all the bad things I have done. I am not what I do—that is my performance. That doesn't mean I'm not guilty or that I don't feel the guilt, remorse, and pain that my actions have caused to myself and others. Beth, all my life I've believed deep down inside that, because of my actions, I was a horrible, no-good, unlovable person. Now, thanks to their help I've learned that God has forgiven my performance and loves me as a person. Now it's possible for me to begin to work on my recovery. As long as I was living in darkness, hating myself, it's doubtful that I would ever have been able to even start to recover. Boy, the way I've rambled on, I bet you're sorry you asked me about RAPHA."

"Not at all; it's good to see you enthused about something. However, I'm a little surprised that you didn't already know some of these things."

"I never knew, or maybe just didn't believe, that God could love a person like me—that he could separate me from my sin. Now, feeling that separation, I truly believe that I have worth as a person! If . . . if this tumor doesn't do me in, I'm sure that applying what I've learned is going to help me in my daily struggle with sexual addiction."

"I know it will!"

"My attorney tells me my date for sentencing will be coming up soon."

"What will happen if they schedule it for a day that you're in the hospital?"

"I'm not sure; I guess they'd have to postpone it. With all the recent programs about child molesters on television, I pray that the judge hasn't been influenced to the point that he changes his mind about my plea bargain!'"

"Doug and I have talked about that, too. The airing of those programs at this time isn't helping you."

Paul laughed. "Oh well, if the doctors tell me I'm going to die of cancer, a jail sentence won't matter very much."

"As you once told me, 'That's stinking thinking!'"

By Friday he had finished painting the bedroom and decided to return home for the weekend. On Monday he would go to the throat specialist. His doctors in Texas had told him that surgery was definitely required. They had also warned him there was a strong possibility that his voice box might have to be removed. Inwardly I flinched, remembering his deep baritone voice and how much he enjoyed singing.

As Paul went out the door, he spoke reassuringly to Doug and me. "No matter what happens, I'll be okay. If I wake up from the surgery, I'll know I'm alive, and if I don't wake up from the surgery, I know I'll be with God."

All weekend Doug and I prayed and fasted. On Monday, after seeing the throat specialist, Paul called and told us that he was being admitted to the hospital the next day; on Wednesday he would have exploratory surgery. The pathological findings of the biopsy done in Texas were inconclusive, so the doctors were planning to do the exploratory and take another biopsy so they would know specifically what type of tumor they were dealing with. Based on their findings, they would then schedule him for additional surgery.

Marie's pastor, his wife, and Shirley went with Marie to the hospital. While Paul was in the operating room, they stayed and prayed with her. Others were praying at home, waiting by the phone to hear how things had gone.

The news was positive! When the surgeon made his incision, he found that the large mass was localized and self-contained. Instantly he knew that he was looking at a large thyroid tumor. After a brief discussion with the other surgeons, he decided not to wait but to immediately remove the tumor along with the entire thyroid gland. As a precaution, in case the tumor was malignant, he also removed a small portion of surrounding muscle tissue. But, praise the Lord, there was no reason to remove the voice box. If the tumor was found to be malignant, Paul would have to undergo chemotherapy, but his doctor was optimistic that the tumor would be benign.

I can only imagine the relief Paul must have felt when he woke up and discovered that the surgery was over, the tumor gone, and that he still had his voice. Now, the only thing left to do was to pray and await the results of the biopsy.

His recovery was so amazingly swift that he was discharged from the hospital after only three days. The week after being discharged, he was well enough to attend a writers' seminar sponsored by our publishing company. Many prayers had been answered!

After an anxious two-week wait, Paul's doctor called and told him the good news—the tumor was benign—he didn't have cancer! The waiting had been difficult, but the good news made it worthwhile.

· 14 ·

Marie's Search for Herself

Search me, O God, and know my heart; test my thoughts.
Point out anything you find in me that makes you sad, and
lead me along the path of everlasting life.
Psalm 139: 23–24

Although Paul's medical crisis was over, the seriousness of his upcoming sentencing weighed heavily on our minds. All decisions for the future were placed on hold. As Paul recuperated from his surgery and Marie continued to work at the nursing home, their lives were in limbo. She was cautious and supersensitive about leaving Ann alone with Paul before his final court appearance, fearful that the Child Welfare Agency might intervene. So while Marie was at work, she left Ann with a nearby Christian family. There were many times when Marie's work schedule required her to stay away overnight, but she made it part of her daily routine to go to the baby-sitter's and help Ann get ready for school.

There were times when the three of them were together as a family. They went through the motions of celebrating Thanksgiving and Christmas, doing the usual festive things for Ann's sake, but their hearts weren't in it. There was just too much turmoil in their lives.

All too soon the holidays were over, and it was the beginning of a new year—time to pack the tinsel and lights away until next Christmas. New presents were quickly forgotten as thoughts turned to other things. For Marie, the past months had caused a buildup of emotions that were about to erupt.

Her counselor knew that the situation was critical. "Marie," she said, "we have to do something to get help for you—now!"

"I've given it to God," she said tearfully. "And I have your help. What more can I do?"

"You need to get away—to a healing environment where counselors can work with you every day."

"You want me to go to RAPHA, don't you?"

"Yes! I'm recommending that you go there for at least thirty days. You know how much they helped Paul. I'm sure they can help you, too. God uses their talents to bring about healing."

"But what about my work . . . and what about Ann?"

"Take a leave of absence. Arrange something with your baby-sitter—you've told me how capable she is. I'm sure you can work something out."

Marie wasn't convinced. "I don't even know if my boss will give me the time off."

"If he doesn't, then maybe you should quit. If you continue like this, you're on your way to a nervous breakdown. If that happens, then you won't be able to work."

"I can't quit. We need the income and I . . . I'll need it even more if I leave Paul."

"Marie, there are always other jobs—but there's only one you. Ask for the time off! I'll ask Bill, our clinic director, to write a letter for you to give to your supervisor."

The nursing home granted her the thirty days off that she requested. Soon Marie was on her way to the same hospital in San Antonio where Paul had been. While she was gone, Ann lived with the baby-sitter's family. Her dad stayed at home, getting up early to pack her lunch, then dropping it off to her before she left to catch the school bus. Doing this gave him an opportunity to see her briefly each day and helped ease her anxieties and fears about her mother's absence. Paul had suffered his whole life from fear of rejection and abandonment, and because of his deep love for his daughter, he didn't want her to go through the same pain.

After seeing Ann safely onto the school bus, Paul would drive to our home and spend the rest of the day working for our company. While living with us, he had become proficient at operating our computer and typesetting equipment. During this time he continued to maintain a daily journal—showing his whereabouts at all times. In a way, Doug and I were still his alibi, but in return, his work in our business proved to be a real blessing.

Every day Marie called Paul from Texas. Based on their conversations, he began to believe that she was recovering. Apparently, they were teaching her how to express her feelings and emotions. She wrote to me several times, and I, too, was encouraged by her words. Her environment sounded like a spiritual haven, and the staff members were treating her wonderfully. They found that although she had difficulty expressing her anger verbally, she could express it through nonverbal art therapy. The rage that her mind wouldn't allow her to express, she was able to share through her drawings. This was extremely helpful for her start on the road to recovery. When she returned from Texas, the same problems would await her. But she would be better equipped to handle them; she felt emotionally and physically stronger.

Through her therapy, Marie began to realize that she hadn't been living life for herself. Instead, she had been living her life through her husband, her individual identity had become totally smothered and enmeshed with his—she had become a codependent. There is a joke that a codependent person who is drowning sees *another* person's life flash before his eyes. That isn't too far wrong, as codependent people live their lives for others and have no identity of their own.

As I read about codependency, I found that most codependent people have low self-esteem and try to be all things to all people. They are not necessarily addicts, but their own core identity is undeveloped. Many times this enables the sexually addicted spouse to act out. Codependent people fear they cannot exist on their own. If codependent people are asked about themselves, they have nothing to say, but they can tell you all about their children, spouse, and others whom they care for. Being indispensable to others and feeling responsible for their actions is the source of codependents' self-worth.

The codependent spouse of a sex addict can become so preoccupied with his sexual problems that it may lead her to try to control his behavior. She watches him continually and demands accountability for every moment of his time. When she comes to the conclusion that all her efforts haven't changed his addictive behavior, she may try even harder. Of course, since the addict is powerless over his problem, all of her efforts to change him are fruitless.

"Enabling, in contrast to controlling, stems from denial and rationalization. Covering up for the addict, protecting him or her from consequences, and keeping silent about personal concerns are the behavioral ingredients of enabling."[1] In most cases enablers don't recognize that it is their actions that allow the addict to continue in his or her addiction. The codependent wife of a sex addict may choose to overlook the obvious problem, minimize it, or attempt to rationalize it away.

Ever since Paul's arrest, I had sensed Marie's denial of her husband's actions. Outwardly, she knew what he had done, but inwardly, she wasn't facing that truth. She knew in her head but not in her heart, and she had to accept the truth before she could move forward in her life.

Dr. Patrick Carnes, author of *Out of the Shadows*, says, "One of the first reactions of a grieving person is the denial of the loss of the loved one. . . . A grieving person resolves pain by acknowledging the loss and reconnecting with others. Losing a loved one to addiction, however, has the potential of keeping one stuck in the early stages of grief, never coming to resolution. The addict is still present in one's life even though the loss of the relationship is real."[2]

The RAPHA staff in Texas had built a foundation in Marie's heart and mind that could be built on with continued therapy from her counselors. She needed to discover who she was as a person, apart from her husband. If her marriage was to be saved, she needed to work on improving her self-image and learn how to think and act independently. She decided to quit her job because of the inordinate amount of stress placed on her by her coworkers when they found out she hadn't left Paul. This allowed her to be at home full-time with Ann—no more baby-sitter. Paul continued to work every day at our publishing company.

⋆ 15 ⋆

The Sentencing

For we speak as messengers from God, trusted by him to tell the truth; we change his message not one bit to suit the taste of those who hear it; for we serve God alone, who examines our hearts' deepest thoughts.
1 Thessalonians 2:4

Finally Paul's sentencing date was set. This would be the moment of truth that would affect him and his family for the rest of their lives. *Oh, God,* I prayed, *please, let the judge accept his plea. Free him from the bondage that's held him captive for so long.*

Once again, Paul told Marie he was going to court alone to face the judge. "I'm the offender," he said. "It's something I want to do by myself."

Doug had taken the day off so we could be with Marie while Paul was in court. We arrived at their home early before Paul had left.

The mood was tense; we were all trying a little too hard to be casual. As Marie prepared water for tea, we observed that her hands were visibly shaking. Paul was in a manic state and talking nonstop. It was as if he believed that words could drown his fears.

Just before it was time for him to leave, the four of us formed a circle and joined hands. Each of us prayed for God to intervene in the courtroom. We prayed for the victims and their families, and asked that the judge be given wisdom and insight in making his decision. Paul wanted and needed help, but for him, jail was not the answer.

Many people believe that the best and only way to protect society from sex offenders is to put them in jail and throw away the key. The following quotes taken from *Retraining Adult Sex Offenders: Methods and Models* were made by well-known experts on this subject. They all contradict the belief that a lifetime in jail is the answer.

Richard Seely, director of the intensive treatment program for sexual aggressives, Minnesota Security Hospital, contends that punishment is a reinforcer to sex offenders, "a reinforcer of his own shame, his own blame, and his own grief, and that serves no purpose."[1]

A. Nicholas Groth, Ph.D., co-director, the sex offenders program, Connecticut Correctional Institution, is convinced that, whatever the degree of risk a pedophile, for instance, poses to the community, ultimately the best protection for society is some form of treatment. "The crime is a symptom; the offense may be punished, but the condition must be treated. The offender must be held responsible for his behavior, but he also has to be helped to change that behavior if we want our community to be a safer one. Otherwise, we are simply recycling him back into the community at the same risk he was prior to incarceration. Incarcerating him is only a temporary solution."[2]

Treatment specialist Robert Freeman-Longo, director of the sex offender unit at Oregon State Hospital, sees prison punishment alone not only as unproductive but as increasing the sex offenders' pathology so that they come out with worse fantasies than before their incarceration. "They come out with more violence, they are more angry, and oftentimes their crimes escalate so that more harm is done to their victims. Prison is not a cure for this problem, and if we are going to use it as a cure, we had better make laws that say, 'You are locked up the rest of your life until you die,' because outside of a specialized treatment for sex offenders, that is the only way to prevent these men from re-offending."[3]

There are, of course, some sex offenders who don't benefit from treatment because they won't change their pattern of behavior no matter what is done. Some have multiple character disorders and don't want to change a way of life that is pleasurable to them. But remember that they comprise only a small percent; most offenders truly desire to change their behavior.

Paul was the last to pray. After asking forgiveness for his sins, he thanked God for his family and the friends who had stood by him. Then, after turning the decision of the judge over to God, he walked out the door.

After he left, we talked about what we might do when he returned. Maybe we'd go out to eat or take a drive in the country. All of us tried not to think of the possibility that he might not return—that he might go from court to jail.

The three of us spent the next few hours sitting around the kitchen table, making small talk in an effort to keep our spirits up. The hands on the kitchen clock moved ever so slowly. Finally, Doug stood up. "I think we should go for a walk. Exercise takes a person's mind off things."

Marie quickly responded to his suggestion. "That's a great idea."

And so we walked—and walked—and walked—up and down every street in the neighborhood. We barely spoke—words weren't necessary to convey our intense feelings. The sights and sounds around us, the birds, flowers, grass, and sky, enhanced our realization that God was present with us, protecting us. Marie had mixed feelings about Paul, but I knew without a doubt that she didn't want him to go to prison. *Marie,* I thought, *reach out—draw your strength and support from God!*

Returning to the house, we sat on the living room sofa catching our breath, drinking tea, and anxiously listening for the sound of Paul's car. It was past noon. *He should be home by now,* I thought.

It seemed as if Marie had heard my thoughts. "The last time he went to court, it took longer than we thought it would. Guess this time is going to be the same."

"He'll be here soon," Doug said.

Twice the phone rang and Marie nervously answered it, but the calls weren't from Paul—just a neighbor and a friend wanting to chat. They weren't aware that Paul was in court.

Watching television and listening to the radio took too much concentration, so we just sat there quietly and prayed—trying to close our minds to any negative thoughts. Suddenly, hearing a car pull into the driveway, Marie stood up and rushed to the picture window. "He's here. He's home!" she said, relief showing on her face.

"Thank you, God," Doug said softly.

"Yes, thank you, God," I echoed.

Paul came into the house looking tired and distraught. "It was terrible," he said, obviously shaken. "I didn't know . . . I just didn't know how ashamed it would make me feel."

"Paul," I said impatiently, "tell us what happened. What was your sentence?"

"They accepted what my attorney suggested. I'll be on probation for two years—but with all kinds of conditions attached. My . . . my life will be an open book, available for my probation officer and the court to examine at any time."

"What conditions?" Marie asked.

"I have to go into a psychiatric hospital for thirty days. The time I spent at RAPHA meets that condition. I've been placed in Bill's sex offender's program, which means that for the next two years I'll have to see him every week for individual counseling and also attend his weekly group sessions for sex offenders. A few weeks ago, Bill told me that if the judge placed me in the offender's program, I'd have to attend at least two twelve-step meetings for sex addicts each week." He caught his breath before continuing. "I'm forbidden to do any volunteer work involving children or be employed where I would have direct contact with children under age eighteen. And, of course, I'm not allowed to have any contact with the victims. And . . . oh yes . . . I almost forgot. I was fined and had to pay courts costs."

"That all seems fair," Doug said.

"It is, but the probation part frightens me. For the next two years, if anyone makes an accusation against me—even a false one—the police will pick me up and I'll go back to jail. The way the court system works, I could be in jail for months before getting the chance to prove that I was innocent. When you're picked up and jailed while on probation, you aren't allowed to post bond—you remain in jail."

"That means you're going to have to be very careful," Doug said. "Sounds like you should continue to keep your activities log and avoid any and all tempting situations."

Doug's words apparently bothered Paul, because his reply sounded fearful. "What if I accidentally see one of the girls in a grocery store or doctor's office? To be safe, will I have to go into hibernation for the next two years?"

Doug made a suggestion. "No, you can't stay away from people, but you might want to consider selling your home and moving to a different town where people won't know about you. That would eliminate any chance of your having contact with one of the girls."

"Hey, you guys are too serious," I said. "We should be celebrating and thanking God for answering our prayers." Looking at Paul, I continued, "You made it through your sentencing, and you're not in jail. God's been with you through all of this, and I'm sure he isn't going to desert you now. Everything will work out."

"Paul, she's right," Marie said. "God is good to us, and we have to believe that he'll continue to be with us."

"Us," Paul repeated softly, looking at his wife. "That's the nicest word I've heard today." Then, after a few more minutes of conversation, he and Doug went out and bought a double cheese and pepperoni pizza smothered in mushrooms. It was our dinner, but it felt like a celebration party—pizza never tasted better.

✦ 16 ✦

Rebuilding a Marriage

*And he and his wife are united so that they are no longer
two, but one. And no man may separate what God has
joined together.*

Mark 10:8–9

I t had become obvious that there would be no instant
healing of Paul and Marie's marriage. They had too
many deeply rooted problems to deal with. At times,
they made a little progress—then inevitably that
progress would be followed by a setback. They argued about
things that didn't matter and ignored the real issues. Marie's
main coping method was to deny the seriousness and
complexity of her husband's sexual addiction. She knew that
he'd done something wrong. She knew that he was on
probation. She knew that he was receiving counseling and

psychiatric help. But she needed to know more! She needed to know and accept that when a person has a sexual addiction, it's a lifetime addiction, a day-to-day struggle. She needed to realize that victory over sexual addiction can come about only by overcoming the temptations.

Unless God supernaturally intervenes, there is no instant cure for Paul's illness. But with God's help, the support of a professional counselor specializing in sexual addiction, and participation in a twelve-step program specializing in sexual addiction, a sex addict can learn how to live with his inappropriate sexual desires. The key words are *learn how to live with*—not cure.

Recovering sex addicts must constantly be aware of their thoughts and actions, carefully avoiding any thought or situation that might trigger a sexual response. To some degree, this constant monitoring intrudes upon and affects the lifestyle of the rest of the family. Therefore, these changes should be discussed openly by family members, striving for a spirit of understanding and cooperation. When this is done, it helps prevent resentment. Should an alcoholic's wife send her husband to the liquor store to buy a bottle of bourbon? Should she give him a beer to drink? Of course not! The point is that, just as it's impossible for a person to be an ex-alcoholic, it's also impossible for a person to be an ex-sexaholic. Once an addict—always an addict. A sex addict in recovery is still a sex addict.

Sexual addiction is Paul's affliction for life. Satan has tried to use this to destroy him and countless others. In recovery, Paul has learned that without God, he is totally powerless— he can do nothing by himself. Every day and in each situation, he puts his trust in God and, as God meets his needs, his faith and ability to trust grow stronger. He has frequent trials and temptations, but he looks on these as a test to his faith. When they come, he can either choose to believe God's promises or come up with his own answers. In the past, his own answers have always failed him. When Paul is tempted, he relies on God's Word to sustain him.

> And God has reserved for his children the priceless gift of eternal life; it is kept in heaven for you, pure and undefiled, beyond the reach of change and decay. And God, in his mighty power, will make sure that you get there safely to receive it, because you are trusting him. It will be yours in that coming last day for all to see. So be truly glad! There is wonderful joy ahead, even though the going is rough for a while down here. These trials are only to test your faith, to see whether or not it is strong and pure. It is being tested as fire tests gold and purifies it—and your faith is far more precious to God than mere gold; so if your faith remains strong after being tried in the test tube of fiery trials, it will bring you much praise and glory and honor on the day of his return.
>
> 1 Peter 1:4–7

Paul believes that God is telling him through this Scripture why he has chosen not to give him an instant and total deliverance from lust. He believes that God is saying that he will find deliverance and an increase in faith only when he relies totally on God each day for his strength and provision. Although God sometimes provides instant deliverance, we must be open to what his will is for us, willing to accept whatever method he chooses for us.

Every month Paul was painfully reminded that he was a sex offender when he went to see his probation officer at the county courthouse. As long as he could go to work and then return home, his life, outwardly, appeared to be normal. However, these visits to the probation office forced him to face the reality that he was indeed a criminal, someone who had nearly gone to jail, and at first they made him extremely depressed. As he sat there waiting his turn with other offenders, he struggled with shame and guilt. He looked around the room at the other people and tried to convince himself that he was different—that he wasn't like them. Many appeared unkempt, angry, and hardened by life; some even looked dangerous. Paul said to himself, *God, I thank you that I'm not like them.* But then the truth would dawn on him that he wasn't any different or better than they were. In fact, if they knew what he had done, they would hate him. His greatest fear was that someone would recognize him. He knew that if this happened, even more shame would overwhelm him. Thank God this never happened.

After what seemed like an eternity, Paul's probation officer would call him into the office. As he answered the questions, Paul found it difficult to remember what he had learned at RAPHA about self-worth and person versus performance. In this setting, he didn't feel very special or that he had much self-worth. Although his probation officer was helpful and kind in dealing with him, overall, the experience was humiliating and humbling.

After every visit he would return home, pick up Marie, and take her out to lunch at their favorite Chinese restaurant. This gave them both something to look forward to on an otherwise bleak day and helped boost their spirits. Eventually, it became a celebration lunch—one more month of recovery—one less month of being on probation.

Marie's counselor advised her to learn more about sexual addiction and recommended several books for her to read. She also told her that it might help if she attended a twelve-step meeting for the spouses of sex addicts where she could get support from other wives whose husbands had similar problems. Marie bought the books but couldn't read them; she felt they were too explicit in describing the various ways in which a sex addict could act out. She needed more time and healing. However, she began to attend the meetings, and they seemed to help. Being able to openly share with these women who understood her situation made her feel less alone. She also learned how much Paul's recovery depended upon his faithfully attending his twelve-step meetings.

For several months, Doug and I watched Ann for them so they could attend their Friday night meetings. As a couple, they were trying to rebuild their marriage—block by block. Twenty-eight years of marriage gave them a foundation to build on, but because it had been weakened by an emotional earthquake, it was unsteady and in danger of collapsing.

By now, Paul was working full-time for our company and proving to be a valuable asset. His organizational skills and knowledge of office procedures prompted us to offer him the position of business director. His God-given talents and previous business experience made him highly qualified for the position.

Marie, too, began to show enthusiasm and interest in our business and began working as a volunteer. When I was invited to speak about publishing in my hometown in West Virginia, I asked her if she would like to go with me to help. She said yes without any hesitation.

During our two days together, I began to see signs that a healing was beginning to take place within her. No longer was she the tense, frightened woman who had gone to RAPHA just a few months earlier. Now she was laughing and responding to people around her. Most important of all, she was beginning to trust again—in God, herself, and life. Acting like a tour guide, I escorted her around town, introduced her to my relatives, and later that evening practiced my speech and had her critique it.

On our second day there, after giving my speech, we returned to our motel room to relax, watch TV, and munch on goodies. There wasn't anything interesting on TV, so we shut it off and began to talk.

"I've had a good time," Marie said. "It's too bad we can't stay longer."

"Me, too. But I'm anxious to get back to Doug and my business."

"Yeah, and I have to get back to Ann."

"And Paul."

"And Paul," she agreed. "But my going back to him isn't the same as your returning home to Doug."

"Aren't things any better between you?"

"At times. But we have so much to overcome! Look what I've gone through since his arrest. In just a few seconds, life as I knew it was gone—taken away from me."

"It must have been devastating for you. Doug and I were shocked. We couldn't believe it. We were sure it had to be a mistake."

"When Paul called me from the jail, I could tell by the sound of his voice that it was true. Thank God, Bill and the counseling center were so close. Without his help and advice, I don't know what would have happened. Ann might have been taken away. I felt as if I were a lead character in a horror movie. It was awful!"

"Did you have an attorney?"

"No. And it's difficult to find one late in the day on Friday. I don't know how many I called without success. Finally, I decided to call every attorney listed in the yellow pages—in alphabetical order. 'God,' I said, 'the first one who agrees to take his case is the one I'll hire.'"

"You didn't know that Paul was a sex addict, did you?"

"No! I didn't. I've honestly searched my mind to see if there were any clues. Over and over I asked myself if there was anything in his past behavior that was suspicious."

"And?"

"If I overlooked something, I didn't do it intentionally. I've always trusted him. If I did anything wrong, it was being too trusting, too gullible. He's been my whole life. He's always been first and I've been second—I've put his wants and needs ahead of mine."

"At least one good thing has come out of all this—you've grown spiritually and mentally."

"But he's hurt me so much. The day after he was put in jail, two detectives came to the house with a search warrant. There's no way to describe the shame I felt as they searched our home, looking in desk and dresser drawers, going through personal things, searching for evidence. I wanted to run away or hide, but there was no place to go. It was awful. Finally when I couldn't stand it any longer I went into my bedroom, turned on my tape player, and sat there listening to Christian music. But there was no escape—they searched that room too. I was angry, frightened, and ashamed, but I couldn't cry. I was helpless; I couldn't do anything."

"Shirley told me that when she came over to see you, within hours of Paul's arrest, you were busy making candles."

"Yes, that's my way of running away—trying to stay busy—trying not to think."

"Did you visit Paul while he was in jail?"

"No. My main concern was for Ann. Bill told me I should immediately take her out of town to a safe place, so I took her to stay with my cousin. I was also busy trying to find bail money for Paul—we needed fifty thousand dollars. He had to get out of there; he'd been threatened and lived in fear for his life. The horror of those days he spent in jail have made a lasting impression on him."

"But, thank God, it's over. Now he won't have to go back. He's in recovery."

"He'd better be. I've told him that I've gone through this once, and I won't go through it again. He knows that he doesn't get a second chance; if it happens again, our marriage is over."

"But if he doesn't slip up—if he learns how to act . . ."

"I'm not making any promises." She turned her eyes away from mine. "It's not just what he was arrested for . . . he . . . he's also had affairs with women."

"How do you know?"

"When he was in the hospital in Texas, I was talking with him and his counselor on a three-way phone conference. I asked Paul if he had ever been sexually involved with other women. His counselor advised me to seriously think about my question and asked me to list the pros and cons of knowing versus not knowing. After doing so, if I still wanted to know, Paul would answer my question. My mind already knew what the answer would be, but my heart didn't want to believe it. That evening when Paul called, I told him I had given it a lot of thought and that I wanted to know the whole truth. The answer hit heavy on my heart. He had been unfaithful to me—not just once—but many times. When I flew to Texas for joint counseling with him during his last three days at RAPHA, we discussed the details. Some of the women he had been with were only acquaintances of mine, but what really hurt me was finding out that one was a woman I considered to be my personal friend."

"Have you forgiven him?"

She laughed. "In a way I have. It was a conditional forgiveness, based on whether he lived or died. Extending an offer of forgiveness to a dying person is one thing—making it stick when they don't die is another."

It was now my turn to laugh. "Do you know what you need?"

"What?"

"To get away for a week—just the two of you—all by yourselves. We'll watch Ann so you can go on a mini-honeymoon and get reacquainted."

"You mean get acquainted. Apparently I've never really known him. I still find it hard to believe that the person I thought I knew so well is a stranger."

"Okay, so even if you do have to start over again, I still think it's a good idea."

"I'm not so sure. Lately, every time we talk, we get into an argument."

"A romantic setting might help. You need time alone."

"Beth, I'm not ready for romance. When I think of him being . . ." she bit her lip. "You have no idea how relieved I was when his test for AIDS came back negative."

"I'm not talking about sex, Marie. I'm talking about courtship. The two of you need to talk, hold hands, go for walks, and take time to communicate and share feelings."

She turned off the lamp. "How's this for communicating? Good-night, Beth."

"Good-night!"

We had a relaxing drive home, and the weather couldn't have been nicer. Marie told me they had been talking about selling their home and moving to an area where people wouldn't know them. They had looked at some homes near the counseling center and were now considering looking at some in our area.

"I can understand why you want to move," I said. "But it's a shame that you have to sell your beautiful home."

"I know; we hate to leave it. I'm sure we'll have difficulty finding another one as nice—unless we pay a small fortune. Houses just aren't selling. It could take months, or longer, to find a buyer. And then what happens if Paul and I separate or divorce?" She sighed. "It's not an easy decision."

"True, but if it's God's plan that you move, why not pray that he sends you a buyer and a new home."

"Lately, I've had difficulty talking to God. My counselor tells me I'm angry with God, but as long as I can tell him about my anger, it's okay. She told me that 'anger turned inward becomes depression!' And I sure don't need any more of that!"

"God understands all of our emotions, including anger. Even if he doesn't always give us a clear explanation for all the why's of life, he gives us the faith to trust him."

"I guess."

A month later, while Ann was at Girl Scout camp for a week, Marie and Paul decided to take the week off and get away together. They had friends who owned a cabin located in a beautiful, scenic part of the state. The owners rarely used it and let them stay there free. It was a gift from God. Since the cabin was located in the wilderness in the northern part of the state, with few houses and no nearby towns, they had plenty of time alone—talking, walking, and simply enjoying nature.

They came back holding hands and acting like newlyweds. They told us they had experienced the beginning of a new closeness and warmth in their relationship—and it showed. Doug and I hoped that what had happened to them would last. But then the reality of everyday life returned and began to destroy the beauty and closeness they had shared. Once more tempers flared, words became weapons, and Marie again began to ask herself if she wanted to stay with Paul.

Not long afterwards, we invited them to go with us to an ethnic food and craft festival in a small town near our home. It was an annual fun event—one where friends, neighbors, coworkers, and strangers could meet and taste ethnic foods, buy crafts, or dance in the street. We were all having a good time until Marie and I decided to leave the others to look at some homemade crafts. She said something that disturbed me and spoiled my festive mood.

As we were fighting the crowd, walking toward the craft booths, she said, "At least no one will recognize me here. We're far enough away from home that I don't have to worry about running into any of Paul's women. We've lived in four different states, but at least this is a part of the country where we aren't known."

"What brought this on all of a sudden?"

"It's not all of a sudden. It's constantly on my mind. I have a feeling that Paul has been with many more women than what he's told me about."

I became impatient. "Marie, you know he's sick! You know he's getting treatment! What difference does it make if there have been more women? Sin is sin! Forgiveness doesn't have a thing to do with numbers. It's his present and future behavior that should concern you, not the past. Women and girls may always be a temptation for him, but it's what he does with those temptations that counts. Think about it. What do you gain if you don't forgive him? What do you lose if you do forgive him?"

She quickly changed the subject. It occurred to me that what she still wanted to believe was that, somehow, he would be totally and instantly cured. Or perhaps she believed that because of his arrest and time in jail, it wouldn't happen again. *If only it were that simple,* I thought.

· 17 ·

The Treatment

*Then they cried to the Lord in their troubles, and he helped
them and delivered them. He spoke, and they were
healed—snatched from the door of death.*

Psalm 107:19–20

As I begin this chapter, dealing with the treatment
of sexual addiction, I want to list specific events in
Paul's life which, according to some experts, might
explain why he made incorrect choices in expressing his sexuality. Remember that the following circumstances are applicable only to Paul's unique situation.

1. His parents married in their teens, and their marriage
   was unstable.

2. His parents divorced when he was four, and the courts granted custody to his maternal grandparents. Although they loved him, treated him well, and met his physical needs, they couldn't meet his emotional needs—to be touched, kissed, and hugged by his mom and dad, to hear his parents tell him that he was wanted and loved.

3. His dad moved away when the divorce became final. A few years later, his mom left to work in another state. He only saw them for a few days each year. Even though his grandparents loved him, he still felt rejected, abandoned, worthless, and unwanted. He believed that he was unlovable.

4. His mother and stepfather were alcoholics, which resulted in physical and emotional abuse.

5. Beginning at age twelve he moved around, first living with one parent and then the other. Summers were spent with his grandparents. As a result, he never established permanency in a relationship.

6. Because his mom and dad left him, he couldn't trust people and developed a domineering and manipulative personality as a defense against being hurt. Also to protect himself, he became an accomplished liar and an expert at conning people. He built walls to keep people out and his shame in.

7. Both his mom and dad exhibited sexual compulsiveness in his presence during his teenage years.

8. As a young boy he was sexually molested many times, which confused his ability to differentiate between love and sex. Through these initial sexual encounters, he finally felt totally accepted for who he was. As a result, throughout his life, he continued to equate his acceptance as a person—his self-worth—with his sexual success. Sex became the reason for his being. Because of his masterful ability to lie, manipulate, con, conceal, and build walls around himself, he was able to successfully lead a double life. He did, however, live in con-

stant fear that his secret life would become known to others.

9. He suffers from bipolar manic-depression. One of the symptoms of this illness is hypersexuality—an abnormal increase in the person's sex drive. Some say that this insatiable sexual appetite in a man is similar to nymphomania in the female.

When Paul was arrested, he was crying for help. He wanted to get caught because he could no longer live with what he was doing. He wanted to change—to be rescued—to save himself and others from his actions.

Paul no longer deceives himself that he will be instantly cured from his sexual addiction. Nor does he profess that a miraculous religious or moral conversion has made him well. He does, however, seek God's help to gain the knowledge and strength necessary to recognize, face, and overcome the many sexual temptations that besiege him every day. He realizes that while other people can advise and help him, ultimately, he is the only one who can overcome and unlearn his destructive behavior patterns. He is accomplishing this by practicing self-discipline and the twelve steps, receiving individual and group counseling, faithfully attending twelve-step meetings for sexual addiction, and living one day at a time. He is working on replacing his false belief system, which laid the foundation for impaired thinking and supported his addictive cycle, with healthy new beliefs. Dr. Patrick Carnes, in his book *Out of the Shadows*, lists four false core beliefs that are held by most, if not all, sex addicts. They are:

Core Belief #1: I am basically a bad, unworthy person.
Core Belief #2: No one would love me as I am.
Core Belief #3: My needs are never going to be met if I have to depend on others.
Core Belief #4: Sex is my most important need.[1]

Paul is learning to see himself as God sees him—a good person who is capable of loving and worthy of being loved. Then he is able to see others differently—as whole persons, not just sexual beings. He knows that sexual activity will never be able to satisfy his need for love and acceptance. His self-worth is now based on who he is in God, not on his sexual ability. He also knows that God has forgiven him for his sins.

Paul receives individual treatment from both a psychiatrist and a competent Christian counselor. Through them he is learning a great deal about himself, including the triggers or sequence of thoughts, feelings, events, and circumstances that precede his acting out. Using this knowledge, he can recognize and turn over to God his inappropriate sexual desires. He knows that this will be a full-time monitoring job for the rest of his life.

Willpower alone cannot keep a sex addict or sex offender sober and in recovery. Intervention techniques are necessary to help break the offensive cycle of acting out. The following techniques used by Paul may also be helpful to other addicts/offenders:

1. When sexual temptation or emotional frustration occurs, he uses the telephone to contact his counselor, sponsor, fellow Sexaholics Anonymous member, or friend.
2. When his mind becomes filled with inappropriate sexual thoughts, he loudly says no or stop. This breaks his thought process and, if done in a public place, is embarrassing. People have given him strange looks—but it's effective.
3. He stops sitting and gets moving; physical exercise seems to help. A brisk walk, a bike ride, a swim—just a change in activity can sometimes help.
4. The cold shower that everybody jokes about actually helps.

5. He thinks about what would happen if he acted out on the temptation. Is this worth five years in jail? Is it worth losing my friends and family? Is it worth losing my job? Is it worth having the world know of my addiction/offense? Is it worth losing my sobriety/recovery? Saying these things out loud to himself also helps.

6. He prays for the person who is the object of his lust. It's difficult to lust and pray at the same time.

7. He tries to place himself in the shoes of the person for whom he is lusting. He tries to feel the fear, shame, and humiliation she would feel if he acted out with her. If he can understand those feelings, he then knows why he shouldn't become sexually involved with her.

8. He practices aversive thinking; whatever he fears or is disgusted by is aversive—snakes, spiders, jail, vomit, pain, etc. Replacing his pleasant, lustful thoughts with unpleasant ones takes him away from lust. After a while this technique becomes almost a conditioned response to a lustful situation.

9. He surrenders his will and temptations to God in prayer, asking for the strength to resist.

10. He faithfully attends twelve-step meetings every week.

Paul says he has never used any of the following drastic techniques, but he is ready to do so rather than become a repeat sex offender:

1. If necessary, he will go into a police station and sit there until his urge to reoffend passes.

2. He will approach the woman who has triggered him and identify himself to her as a sex offender. If the person is a child, he will turn and *run*, not walk away.

3. If necessary, he will commit a minor crime, (e.g., break a window). It's better to pay a fine and go to jail for a few days than to reoffend and go to jail for years.

One evening while doing dishes, I overheard Paul discussing these intervention techniques with Doug.

"Paul, what you're saying is interesting, but those techniques could be used by anyone, not just a sex addict. In fact, Joseph in the Old Testament used similar methods when Potiphar's wife tried to seduce him."

Paul laughingly agreed. "The way she chased him, he probably went swimming in the river several times a day just to cool off! Imagine having a powerful, wealthy, and attractive young woman say to you several times each day, 'I want you to sleep with me.'"

"You're probably right; they didn't have cold showers back then," Doug said. "But, you know, Joseph did stop and think about what the consequences would be if he did what she wanted. Poor Joseph, there he was, a trusted slave in the woman's house, owned by her husband—the captain of Pharaoh's guards. Talk about consequences! Going to bed with her would have been stupid; he would have gone to jail or maybe even been killed."

"I think Joseph was more concerned about the consequences of the sin in God's eyes. God had been with him through all kinds of adversity, and he didn't want to change that close relationship by committing the sin of fornication. But, even though he repeatedly told her no, she didn't give up. If you ask me, she was either a nymphomaniac or a sex addict!"

"She was also a scorned woman who screamed 'rape'—or attempted rape. Even though he was innocent, her lies sent Joseph to jail."

"Doug, you'd be surprised at the number of false accusations that are made. It happens all the time. And being a sex offender on probation makes me an open target for the same thing. I'm fair game to anyone who doesn't like me or what I've done. I don't know which I fear the most—reoffending or a false accusation."

"Paul, you sound paranoid. But I agree that you should be careful and protect yourself. Joseph was a slave and couldn't protect himself—but you can."

Like Joseph, Paul is acutely aware that he can't run away from or avoid sexual temptations, but he can, and must, avoid intentionally putting himself in the path of those temptations. Because of his attraction to young girls, he must:

1. Never allow himself to be unchaperoned with a young girl for any extended period of time.
2. Avoid playgrounds, swimming pools, parks, and other places where young girls congregate, unless he is accompanied by an adult—preferably one aware of his sexual addiction.
3. Never seek or accept employment that involves working with, or brings him into contact with, young girls.
4. Use caution when establishing a new friendship and carefully monitor any existing friendship if it involves a single parent or couple with a young daughter. Such a friendship should be reassessed and, if there is temptation for him, the relationship should be terminated.
5. Never, under any circumstances, baby-sit or take care of a young girl.
6. Structure his time carefully.
7. Never fully trust himself with a young girl.

Paul also shared some general boundaries that he has established for himself as a sex addict who is attracted to adult women. They can be applied to any adult relationship but are particularly true in sexual addiction. As a sex addict he believes he must:

1. Never be alone for an extended period of time with a woman to whom he feels attracted.

2. Never engage in excessive touching, hugging, etc.
3. Never establish a relationship or be alone with a woman who is hurting, lonely, or vulnerable.
4. Avoid lowering his inhibitions through the use of drugs and alcohol.
5. Avoid watching sexually suggestive television programs or looking at any type of pornography, including R- and X-rated movies.
6. Avoid cruising, crowds, certain stores, and other areas of temptation.
7. Structure his time carefully.
8. Never fully trust himself or his sexuality.

A twelve-step program for sexual addiction, based on the Alcoholics Anonymous program, has played an important role in Paul's recovery. An individual who honestly works the twelve steps can interrupt and alter his impaired thinking, his destructive and compulsive behavior, and his faulty beliefs about self-worth. Although there are a number of self-help groups that deal with sexual addiction, Paul's counselor specifically referred him to Sexaholics Anonymous. He felt that they would be the most helpful for him because of their belief that any form of sex with oneself or with a partner, other than the addict's heterosexual spouse, is progressively addictive and destructive. Other groups are less restrictive. For example, they may consider addicts to be sexually sober and in recovery if they are involved in a homosexual or unmarried heterosexual relationship to which they are committed. Or they may ask what specific sexual problems the person wants help with and then work only on those particular issues.

Through Paul's twelve-step program, he soon realized that he wasn't alone—there were other sex addicts in the world. These people understood his shame, guilt, lust, and frustration; they related to his anger, resentment, fears, fantasies, loneliness, self-hatred, and pain; they reinforced that he wasn't a bad person, that he shared a common illness with them called "sexual addiction." Through working the twelve steps, new beliefs gradually began to replace old ones. First, he learned to trust God; now he's learning to trust people.

The Twelve Steps as Adapted for Sex Addicts

1. We admitted we were powerless over lust—that our lives had become unmanageable.
2. Came to believe that a Power greater than ourselves could restore us to sanity.
3. Made a decision to turn our will and our lives over to the care of God *as we understood God.*
4. Made a searching and fearless moral inventory of ourselves.
5. Admitted to God, to ourselves, and to another human being the exact nature of our wrongs.
6. Were entirely ready to have God remove all these defects of character.
7. Humbly asked God to remove our shortcomings.
8. Made a list of all persons we had harmed, and became willing to make amends to them all.
9. Made direct amends to such people wherever possible, except when to do so would injure them or others.
10. Continued to take personal inventory and when we were wrong promptly admitted it.
11. Sought through prayer and meditation to improve our conscious contact with God, *as we understood God,* praying only for knowledge of God's will for us and the power to carry that out.
12. Having had a spiritual awakening as the result of these Steps, we tried to carry this message to other sex addicts, and to practice these principles in all our affairs.

The Twelve Steps of Alcoholics Anonymous

1. We admitted we were powerless over alcohol — that our lives had become unmanageable.
2. Came to believe that a Power greater than ourselves could restore us to sanity.
3. Made a decision to turn our will and our lives over to the care of God *as we understood Him.*
4. Made a searching and fearless moral inventory of ourselves.
5. Admitted to God, to ourselves and to another human being the exact nature of our wrongs.
6. Were entirely ready to have God remove all these defects of character.
7. Humbly asked Him to remove our shortcomings.
8. Made a list of all persons we had harmed, and became willing to make amends to them all.
9. Made direct amends to such people wherever possible, except when to do so would injure them or others.
10. Continued to take personal inventory and when we were wrong promptly admitted it.
11. Sought through prayer and meditation to improve our conscious contact with God, *as we understood Him*, praying only for knowledge of His will for us and the power to carry that out.
12. Having had a spiritual awakening as the result of these Steps, we tried to carry this message to alcoholics, and to practice these principles in all our affairs.

God tells us in Genesis 2:18, "It isn't good for man to be alone; I will make a companion for him, a helper suited to his needs." God first created man and then woman so they could become one. However, it was also in his plans that, even after they became one, they were still to be strong individual people. Just as Eve was Adam's companion, so also is Marie a companion and helper to Paul. It's important that she have faith in him so she can offer encouragement as he rebuilds faith in himself. As his companion, it's also important to her that she share her personal hurts and fears with him, but not blame him for them. A healthy intimate relationship is only possible when two people risk rejection by trusting one another enough to reveal their innermost thoughts and feelings. This communication builds trust, affirms the relationship, and shows responsibility by each for their own actions and feelings. It also strengthens the marriage through the sharing of common problems and helps interrupt the addictive system.

As mentioned earlier, a sex addict's wife is greatly affected by her husband's illness. Paul began using intervention techniques and the twelve-step program to change his way of thinking and acting. This, in turn, changed his lifestyle—a change Marie has to acknowledge and support if her marriage is to survive. If she remains codependent or an enabler, she will continue trying to assume responsibility for his actions— or for covering them up. As a wife, companion, and helper, the opposite is true; she is changing with him and encourages him to accept responsibility for the consequences of his actions. She doesn't allow herself to be conned by any attempts he may make at rationalizing or minimizing his behavior. As difficult as it might be, she needs to learn as much as possible about sexual addiction so she can discuss it intelligently with her husband and her counselor. She also needs to read the books her counselor recommends and, most of all, talk with and question Paul about his addiction, feelings, and fears.

Marie has to be careful not to unwittingly provide her husband with an opportunity to act out. Her situation is even more complicated because of their young daughter. Whenever Ann has a girlfriend over to spend the night, Paul stays in his bedroom watching TV—away from the girls. When Ann's friends come over for the day, they as a couple ensure that he is never alone with them for any length of time. When Ann joined an all-girl soccer team, Paul didn't attend a single practice session or game without his wife by his side. When they go to the beach and the sight of a scantily clad woman or girl bothers him, he can and does freely express his feelings to Marie. Once he tells Marie that something is triggering him sexually, she doesn't become upset. His honesty, openness, and willingness to share these feelings with her is a good indication that he is actively working his program. It's essential that he share his temptations with her because, in doing so, it represents a victory over lust. If he hides his feelings from her or lies to her about them, he will, once again, start living the secret double life of a sex addict. (For single people and those married people who are unable, for whatever reason, to share with their spouse, Paul suggests that they communicate closely with their twelve-step sponsor.)

Whenever Marie hires a baby-sitter to take care of Ann, she has to remember Paul's addiction. It's not always possible to find a competent, grandmotherly type. At times, she has had to hire a young girl. When that happens, she and Paul have an understanding that he will never be the one who drives the girl home. Before hiring the girl, they have a major decision to make. Should they, or should they not, tell her parents about Paul's arrest? If they don't, and the parents eventually find out, they will undoubtedly be very angry. However, if they are told in advance they might say, "Forget it! Our daughter isn't sitting for you. Find someone else." But, then again, they might appreciate the honesty and show understanding.

Whenever Marie invites an adult woman friend to stay overnight at her home, she again has to consider Paul's addiction. He might be tempted by any woman, but if she is unmarried, having a problem with her marriage, under stress, or suffering from low self-esteem, her presence and potential availability would present an even greater temptation. When a woman does stay overnight, it is in a controlled environment with prearranged boundaries that Paul and Marie have discussed prior to the guest's arrival. There is an added danger if the woman has a young daughter with her, particularly if that daughter is lonely, seeking affection, or has been abused. Under no circumstances should Paul ever be alone with a child who has suffered physical, emotional, or sexual abuse.

Some of Paul's self-imposed restrictions also affect Ann, who is sometimes confused by these changes in the family lifestyle. However, she is a bright, sensitive child, and I am convinced that one day she will understand and respect the courage shown by her parents during this crisis.

✦ 18 ✦

In Recovery

Now glory be to God who by his mighty power at work within us is able to do far more than we would ever dare ask or even dream of—infinitely beyond our highest prayers, desires, thoughts, or hopes.
Ephesians 3:20

Recovery is a spiritual journey to the very core of the sex addict's being, which leads to self-discovery. With God's help, the addict strives for progress, not perfection. This journey isn't easy; it's not just a matter of reading the right books, seeing a specific therapist, or joining the right support group. Those are only the external things that can help to bring about an internal healing—a reconnecting of body and soul. Only with God's help and love can an addict come to realize that his or her sexual acting out is the result of bad programming and that he or she is a good, lovable person.

Acknowledging the power of his addiction, Paul has established boundaries—self-imposed restrictions—for himself and his behavior. For now, these restrictions are needed, but as he grows spiritually and has more time in recovery, he hopes he can be less restrictive with himself.

There are definite signs that Paul is in recovery. His treatment started when he took step one and admitted that he was powerless over his lustful sexual behavior and that his life had become unmanageable. He then took steps two and three in which he acknowledged his belief that God would restore him to sanity if he turned his will and life over to him.

Although Paul asked God many times to deliver him from his addiction, he believes his petitions were not honored because he had never completely surrendered his will to God. He needed to be willing to do whatever God asked of him and, in turn, allow God to do whatever he wanted to with him. When Paul begged for help, there was still too much pride, too much ego, too much of himself, crowding God out of his life.

When a person tries to pour milk into a full container, it will spill because there is no room for it. If the container is half-full of vinegar, the milk poured into it will sour. However, if the container is empty, it will hold the milk and not make it sour. Paul's vessel had to be completely empty of himself and his self-will before it could be filled with the working power of God. Only when he hit bottom was he able to reach the point of total surrender. At one of his twelve-step meetings, Paul saw two signs:

Edging God Out = EGO
and
Let Go and Let God

If a person on the first floor wanted to get to an office on the twentieth floor, he or she would use an elevator. But what if the only elevator door in the building that would open was in the basement? Would that person be willing to climb up twenty flights of stairs to reach the destination, or would he or she walk down one flight of stairs to where the elevator door was working? Sometimes, a person has to go down before he or she can move up.

Paul, being human, had been trying to reach God by telling him what to do, according to Paul, without giving up any of his control. But God was waiting for Paul to let go of that control so he could reach down and help him. When Paul allowed God to take his rightful place in his life, it was as if God put his arms around him and gave him the strength that he needed for his daily walk.

From the moment of his arrest, Paul accepted responsibility for what he had done, but at times he tried to downplay or minimize the seriousness of his addiction. For example, he would say, "I'm not the only one! Lots of people do what I did; they just haven't been caught yet. As long as they don't get caught and no one finds out what they've done, they're considered good people." By maintaining sexual sobriety and continuing in recovery, his thinking became clearer and clearer. Now he is embarrassed that he made those statements; he says, "There is absolutely no excuse for what I did."

Paul has empathy for his victims because he fully understands the emotional damage he has caused. He prays for healing—theirs and his. Paul would like to say, "I'm cured and I promise I'll never do those things again," but he realizes he can never truthfully do so. There is no cure for sexual addiction. He is aware that, for the rest of his life, his flesh will be at war with his spirit. He must continually monitor his every thought and action. Many times he has shared his doubts and fears with others. That is good; that is reality.

One day I asked Paul if he had ever considered moving to another state when his probation was over. "No, not really," he replied. "Where I'm living now is probably the safest place for me to be. The police know about me, and they'll be watching me. Also, all the people who know about my arrest will be watching. Having people around who know about me is good; they'll serve as a constant reminder. Beth, there isn't anything that I wouldn't do or go through to keep from reoffending."

"I believe you," I said. And I did!

Paul is sincere in trying to reach out through the twelve-step program to others who, like him, suffer from sexual abuse or addiction. God is opening doors for him in his efforts to help, and this is just the beginning!

The other day my daughter, Tina, called from work. That morning her dad had followed her to a state inspection station where she had left her car for inspection. He then drove her to work.

"Mom," she said. "I'm desperate! My car's at the inspection station, and I can't find anyone to take me there to get it. By the time Dad gets here from work, they'll be closed. I'm really in trouble! I need my car by tomorrow so I can drive my boss to an out-of-town cosmetology show. What am I going to do?"

"Honey, I'd come and get you if I could. But remember, I don't have my car. Your brother took it back to college with him."

"I know, but I was hoping one of our neighbors could come and get me. Will you ask them?"

I thought for a moment. "Honey, I just thought of someone who can help. He'll be there in about thirty minutes."

I knew that our neighbors were either working or not at home, so I asked Paul.

Without hesitation, he agreed. "But, Beth," he said, "shouldn't you call Tina back and let her know that it's me who's coming for her?"

"I'll call her," I said, knowing she had no fear of him.

We didn't speak of trust, but we both knew! As Paul walked toward the door, his thankful, confident smile said it all.

Did I believe he was in recovery? Yes! Had my daughter been thirteen instead of twenty-one, would I have asked him? No! But if she had been thirteen, I am convinced that Paul would have said no too. Why? Because I have witnessed his determined steps toward recovery and have observed God at work in his life.

If you were sexually abused as a child, if you have sexually abused children, or if you are addicted to any kind of sexual activity, remember, you are not alone—help is available to those who want it. If you truly want to change, we suggest you contact one of the sources listed in the appendix. You may choose to ask your pastor, physician, or a social worker where you can obtain care. But make sure you go to a professional who has specialized training in sexual addiction/sexual offending. Also, if your problem involves sexual activity with a minor and you seek help from a psychiatrist, psychologist, counselor, or other professional, make sure that you fully understand that under the child protection laws there is, in most cases, no guarantee of professional confidentiality. In most states, they are required by law to report such sexual activity to the proper authorities. This obviously will get you into trouble with the law, but it will also stop you from hurting any more children—and yourself. It will start you on the road to getting help and put an end to your miserable secret life. The fact that you turned yourself in willingly, instead of waiting to get caught, is usually taken into consideration by the authorities in their determination of punishment. If you are not prepared to possibly go to jail for your actions, then seek help through a twelve-step program for sex addicts or some other confidential source that will maintain your anonymity. But please, get help!

Epilogue

It has been almost three years since Paul's arrest. In that time, he and Marie have continued to struggle in their quest to rebuild their marriage. He takes one day at a time as he works his steps in recovery and faithfully attends his twelve-step meetings for sex addicts every week. His period of probation has been completed, and although he's no longer required by law to do so, he continues to see Bill for individual and group therapy.

Paul has become active in a local church where he now assumes a leadership position in a special ministry dealing with Adult Children of Alcoholics and others who come from dysfunctional homes. Before becoming involved in this ministry, he made the decision to meet privately with the pastor and inform him of his arrest. Paul also provided the pastor with a pre-published copy of the manuscript of this book. The pastor responded with Christian love and welcomed him into the program.

Paul and Marie recently celebrated their thirtieth wedding anniversary, a very positive milestone in their relationship. Pray for them and the millions of others who suffer from the thorn of sexual abuse.

A Professional Perspective

Herbert Hays, M.A., C.C.C.
Director of the Sexual Offenders, Sexual Abuse, and Sexual
   Addiction Programs
Ministries of Eden, Inc., Christian Counseling Center
   (An affiliate of RAPHA Hospitals)
Ford City, Pennsylvania 16226

E very parent, Sunday school teacher, pastor, church
leader, school teacher, and all others who have
intimate contact with children and adolescents
should read this book. Our children are at risk to
be sexually exploited in our schools, churches, and while
participating in activities such as the Boy Scouts, Girl Scouts,
or other youth groups. They are also at risk in the very
communities where they live and play. This risk is increased
by uneducated, unknowing parents and other adults who
supervise and care for children. The information covered in
this book, when read and understood by such parents and
adults, can drastically reduce the risk factor. First, however,
they must accept the fact that their children are being targeted
by sex offenders.

As a therapist who works every day with sex offenders and
their victims, I have come to believe that the majority of our

children—somewhere and sometime—are the targets of sex offenders. They may not actually have been offended at that time simply because the offender did not think that there was a safe opportunity to do so. The offenders I work with are fathers, stepfathers, grandfathers, uncles, Sunday school teachers, and everyday workers who have access to our children in their homes, churches, and communities. An offender, in most cases, is not distinguishable from other people whom we trust our children with at church, Little League practice, and in our social relationships. Many offenders sexually abuse their own children or their stepchildren. This is a more common occurrence than most people would like to admit.

My intent in writing this is to truthfully inform readers of the facts—not to create an exaggerated sense of alarm that would cause us to suspect that every person who has contact with our children is a child molester. But on the other hand, to think that the millions of children who are offended every year are *exceptions* is just sheer ignorance of the profusion of the offenses and is very dangerous to the safety of our children. My own paraphrase of Proverbs 11:14 reads: "Where there is no guidance from those who have experience, the people will fall victim to the victimizer, but there is a way to avoid such a fall, and that is to heed the words of the many counselors who warn of the evil." The things Paul learned, as described in this book, evolved from the research of many counselors who are warning the readers of the evil of child victimization by the sex offender.

There is no profile of a sex offender. There are types of sex offenders such as the incest sex offender, the pedophile, and the rapist, and there are subtypes in each group. It is the nonviolent incest offender and the nonviolent pedophile who offends children the most often. I distinguish between them only for identification purposes, because both types are child molesters who exploit children. By definition both are pedophiles but, based on whom they offend, they are different. The incest sex offender normally offends within his or her own family, while the pedophile normally offends outside his or her own family. Both types are fully capable of offending outside of their normal offending environment. In other words, the incest offender could offend his best friend's daughter, and the pedophile could offend within his own family.

Both types of offenders are rapists in that they use their power and position to sexually exploit children for their own sexual gratification. However, they are different than the forceful rapist in that they do not usually threaten physical violence to gain their victims' compliance to their demands. The methods of the nonviolent molester are, more commonly, coercion, bribery, opportunistic advantage, manipulation, and threats of loss such as the loss of a parent, financial loss, or loss of freedom to the victim. Statements such as the following are commonly used by perpetrators to prevent their victims from disclosing the sexual abuse:

I'll go to jail and then who will be here to take care of you and your mom?

You'll be taken away and will have to live with strangers in a foster home or an orphanage!

Our family will break up and it will be all your fault!

Sometimes the perpetrator pays off the victim by treating him or her more special than others, or by giving presents to the victim that others do not receive. These are only a few of the methods of coercion that are used by perpetrators of incest and by the pedophiles in our communities. It is important to remember that a particular character trait or any one given behavior or activity is not necessarily indicative of possible sexual abuse.

Although Paul in this book is both a sex offender and a sex addict, not all sex offenders are sex addicts. It is also important to understand that not all sex addicts are sex offenders.

Yet, in dealing with these offenders, I have found that incest perpetrators and pedophiles are addicted to the sexual experience with their victims. Most sex addicts who are also sex offenders use various sexual practices that stimulate and aid them in their sexual offending behaviors. Some are addicted solely to their victims and have no compulsive desire to use pornography, visit prostitutes, utilize massage parlors, or engage in voyeurism, exhibitionism, or compulsive masturbation. Although Paul may have had multiple victims, this is not necessarily true of all child sex offenders. Some may have only one or possibly two victims. Paul, like many perpetrators of child sexual abuse, was himself sexually abused as a child. However, not all who were abused offend, and not all who offend were abused. Some come from homes and environments void of any abuse. The urge to satisfy sexual desires is a strong siren in sex offenders and, if they are sexually attracted to children, they can become dangerous predators of children.

Sex offenders can be treated for their offending behavior. It is not an easy or a short course of treatment. However, the sex offender must be treated for the safety of our children—for the safety of our communities. Many alcoholics are successfully rehabilitated, yet others may continue to drink and go out and hurt others. So, too, a sex offender may fail to be rehabilitated and may go out to re-offend and hurt other children. However, if the offender receives no treatment, it is practically guaranteed that other children will be hurt. Offenders such as Paul have a long road to recovery ahead of them, including many years of treatment and a lifetime commitment to the relapse prevention program. When offenders stay committed to relapse prevention for the rest of their lives, they have a very low risk of re-offending. However, if they do not remain committed and begin to think that they are cured, their risk of re-offending is very high.

It is my experience that the relapse prevention model is the most effective model for the treatment of sex offenders. Some can be treated successfully without incarceration and with minimal risk to their communities, while others must be incarcerated and then continue in treatment after they return to their communities. These treatment decisions of when, where, and how are difficult and should be made only by professionals who have experience and specific training in the treatment of sex offenders. All sex offenders, whether guilty of one offense or hundreds of offenses, must receive specific treatment. The treatment of sex offenders is a special field of counseling and should never be undertaken by therapists or counselors who do not have the specialized training necessary to treat such individuals. Doing so could place the community at risk since they do not understand the complicated needs, behaviors, and beliefs of the sex offender. Failure to provide proper treatment to an offender means that more children will be victimized and suffer from the many effects of sexual abuse.

I am convinced that the statistics I see do not begin to tell the real story concerning the prevalence of child sexual abuse. Many children choose not to tell of their abuse. Since the time of Beth's abuse, there has been an increase in the public's awareness and response to this issue, but many parents and/or other adults still fail to report the victimization of children for various reasons.

> Parents may not want their child to be exposed as a victim. As children they, too, may have been victims of abuse and fear the experience of exposing their own emotions.
>
> They may fear the behavior or loss of their spouses.
>
> They may have shame and guilt and are afraid of how their friends, relatives, and neighbors will respond.
>
> They may fear the loss of income and security for their children and themselves.

Although many of their reasons may, on the surface, seem to make sense, in reality it is exactly this kind of thinking that protects a whole host of sex offenders just like Beth's offender—Mr. Stephens. These unidentified, unexposed, unadjudicated, and untreated sex offenders are victimizing our children on an ongoing basis because we have not intervened to expose them. If a sex offender is not properly reported, every child that he subsequently offends becomes our victim, too, because we have protected him with our silence.

Many young victims of sexual abuse are hurt as much from the experience of seeing their offender go unpunished by the system as from the abuse itself. Sex offenders must be punished and treated—both are necessary. Punishment need not be prison or jail, but some form of punishment is a rightful act toward the offender. Treatment is also a rightful and necessary act toward the offender.

I hope that every reader of *The Thorn of Sexual Abuse* becomes bolder and more committed to stamping out the sexual exploitation of children by taking a courageous stand to expose sex offenders, particularly those who offend children. Every offender who is exposed saves a child—possibly many children—from the trauma and torture of sexual exploitation.

Sources of Help

Organizations that may be of help to you:

Sexaholics Anonymous (SA)
P.O. Box 300
Simi Valley, California 93062
Phone: (818) 704-9854

S-Anon
P.O. Box 5117
Sherman Oaks, California 91413
Phone: (818) 990-6910

Augustine Fellowship, Sex and Love Addicts Anonymous (SLAA)
P.O. Box 119, New Town Branch
Boston, Massachusetts 02258
Phone: (617) 332-1845

Sex Addicts Anonymous (SAA) and
Adult Children of Sex Addicts Anonymous (ACSA)
P.O. Box 3038
Minneapolis, Minnesota 55403
Phone: (612) 339-0217

National Association on Sexual Addiction Problems (NASAP)
22937 Arlington Avenue, Suite 201
Torrance, California 90501
Phone: (213) 546-3103

Adults Molested as Children United
Parents United/Daughters and Sons United
P.O. Box 952
San Jose, California 95108
Phone: (408) 280-5055
   Adults Molested as Children United helps to resolve problems of low self-esteem, anger, and guilt often experienced by the victims of sexual abuse. Parents United/Daughters and Sons United is a national self-help organization with many local groups throughout the United States. They provide assistance to families involved in child sexual abuse and also sponsor self-help groups for adults who were sexually abused as children.

National Child Abuse Hotline
Phone: (800) 422-4456
   The National Child Abuse Hotline handles crisis calls and provides information and referrals to every state and county in the United States.

Alcoholics Anonymous
A. A. World Services, Inc.
Box 459, Grand Central Station
New York, New York 10163
Phone: (212) 686-1100

RAPHA
Corporate Offices
8876 Gulf Freeway, Suite 340
Houston, Texas 77017
Phone: (800) 227–2657
   RAPHA has inpatient and outpatient programs available in cities throughout the United States. For information about the program and the treatment center nearest to your area call the above toll-free number.

Notes

Chapter Nine

1. Patrick Carnes, Ph.D., *Out of the Shadows* (Minneapolis: CompCare Publishers, 1983), 9.

Chapter Ten

1. Anna C. Salter, *Treating Child Sex Offenders and Victims* (Newbury Park, Calif.: Sage Publications, 1988), 10–11.

2. Fay Honey Knopp, *Retraining Adult Sex Offenders: Methods and Models* (Orwell, Vt.: Safer Society Press, 1984), 9.

3. Carnes, *Out of the Shadows*, 45.

4. Timothy H. Smith, *You Don't Have to Molest That Child* (Chicago: National Committee for Prevention of Child Abuse, 1987), 3–4.

5. Knopp, *Retraining Adult Sex Offenders*, 10.

Chapter Eleven

1. Salter, *Treating Child Sex Offenders and Victims* (Newbury Park, Calif.: Sage Publications, 1988), 34.

Chapter Twelve

1. Salter, *Treating Child Sex Offenders and Victims*, 231.

Chapter Thirteen

1. Knopp, *Retraining Adult Sex Offenders*, 7.

Chapter Fourteen

1. Carnes, *Out of the Shadows*, 97.
2. Ibid., 88.

Chapter Fifteen

1. Knopp, *Retraining Adult Sex Offenders*, 16.
2. Ibid.
3. Ibid., 15–16.

Chapter Seventeen

1. Carnes, *Out of the Shadows*, 138–43.

DATE DUE

JUN 1 5 1998			